Reich

Modern Masters

Editor: Frank Kermode

Reich

Charles Rycroft

Fontana/Collins

First published in Fontana 1971
Copyright © Charles Rycroft 1971
Printed in Great Britain
for the Publishers Wm. Collins Sons & Co Ltd,
14 St James's Place, London, S.W.1,
by Richard Clay (The Chaucer Press), Ltd,
Bungay, Suffolk

Contents

1 Biographical Introduction

Although this is not a biography of Reich, some facts of his life have to be mentioned if we are to understand his ideas and place them correctly in history. Reich was born on March 24th, 1897, at Dobrzynica in Galicia but spent most of his childhood on a farm at Jujinetz in Bukowina. Both Galicia and Bukowina were outlying provinces of the Austro-Hungarian Empire until its collapse at the end of the First World War, and Reich was therefore an Austrian citizen (until he became a naturalized American in 1938), but one whose home country was abroad from 1919 onwards.

His family was of Jewish origin, but the Jewish religion and observances played no part in his upbringing. His father was a farmer and, according to Ilse Ollendorf Reich, the family was 'well-to-do, highly respected, somewhat stuck-up and put a very pronounced stress on German culture'. They must then, given the current distinction between master nations and subject peoples prevailing within the Austro-Hungarian Empire, have been representatives if not exactly of an occupying ruling class isolated among colonials, at least of a cultural élite which looked north and westwards to Berlin and Vienna for its inspirations. Again according to Ilse Ollendorf Reich, Reich was not allowed to associate with either the local Ukrainian-speaking peasantry or the few Yiddish-speaking Jewish families that lived near by. He seems to have had a lonely childhood, never even becoming intimate with his only brother, who was three years younger than himself.

However—and his followers make something of this —from his earliest years he was in intimate touch with nature, familiar with the details of the farmyard and cattle breeding, and he learnt young to ride and shoot. In this—and in his totally non-Jewish secular upbringing— his childhood was in striking contrast to that of the majority of the intellectuals who were drawn towards psychoanalysis in the 1920s.

Although Reich, one gathers, always spoke nostalgically of the physical surroundings of his childhood and retained throughout his life a great affection and feeling for the countryside, he rarely mentioned his family or reminisced about his childhood, which is hardly surprising in view of the fact that the conjunction of private tragedy and political catastrophe led while he was in his teens to the complete disruption of the whole world he had been brought up in. In 1911, when he was fourteen, his mother committed suicide, apparently after he had revealed to his father that she was having an affair with his tutor. Then his father developed tuberculosis and died three years later. Although Reich was still a schoolboy, he attempted to run the family farm until it became a battlefield. In 1916 he left home and joined the Austrian army, in which he became an officer and saw active service in Italy.

At the end of the war Reich arrived in Vienna, a twenty-one-year-old war veteran, both of his parents dead and his childhood home, which he never visited again, cut off from him by the new frontiers drawn by the politicians at Versailles. After a brief flirtation with the law he became a medical student and decided almost immediately to take up psychiatry. Within a year of arriving in Vienna he became a member of the Vienna

Psychoanalytical Society and a practising psychoanalyst.

To anyone familiar with the contemporary psycho-analytical scene it seems almost incredible that a medical student still in his early twenties should have been allowed to treat patients, or that Reich should have been able to write and get published four papers on psychoanalysis and sexology within three years of his first contact with psychoanalysis. But the psychoanalytical movement was very different then. It had yet to institutionalize training or to insist on a training analysis of several years duration for all would-be analysts, and Reich was far from being the only medically unqualified person who had patients referred to him by Freud within a few months of first coming into contact with psychoanalysis.[1]

It should be mentioned here that Reich contributed significantly to the developments in psychoanalysis which transformed it from what in retrospect appears as an amateurish activity into a professional technique that can be taught formally. From 1924 to 1930 he was the director of the Seminar for Psychoanalytic Therapy, in which practical problems of treatment were thrashed out, and three of his papers on technique are included in a volume called *The Psychoanalytic Reader* (ed. Robert Fliess) which is to this day recommended reading for students at psychoanalytical institutes.

And Vienna in the 1920s was very unlike the affluent societies in which contemporary psychoanalytical

1. Although Reich became an analyst before experience of being a patient was a required part of every analyst's training, he had more than one period of being analysed by more than one analyst. Speaking of his first analysis, Ilse Ollendorf Reich says, 'this analysis was broken off by Reich unfinished, as were the following ones', but of a later analysis in Berlin she reports that it ended abruptly when his analyst emigrated to America.

9

organizations flourish and can exert considerable control over their students' activities. The former metropolis of a large polyglot empire had suddenly become the capital of a small and impoverished republic. The glory and the tinsel had departed with the Hapsburgs; the hierarchical, largely Catholic, feudal structure of society had collapsed, leaving a void waiting to be filled. It is therefore not surprising that Reich became involved in politics, and he was indeed far from being the only analyst who sought to reconcile psychoanalysis and marxism. He seems however to have been the only one whose activities so antagonized both schools of thought that he was expelled from both the International Psychoanalytical Association and the Communist Party.

In view of the fact that the history of the psychoanalytical movement has excited more later curiosity than has that of the German and Austrian communist parties, and that Reich has left more of a mark on psychoanalysis and psychotherapy than on marxism, more explanations are current as to why Reich became unacceptable to the analysts—or broke with them—than of why he was expelled from the communist movement. According to Reich himself, his expulsion was due to theoretical differences regarding the social implications of psychoanalysis, compounded by professional jealousies, but according to others the cause was more personal. Reich wished to be analysed by Freud; Freud refused, Reich took his refusal as a personal rejection, became depressed and tuberculous and even, according to his first wife (but his third wife disagrees), the victim of a 'deteriorating process', from which he never recovered.

If this second explanation is correct, developing a father-fixation on Freud with resulting therapeutic longings towards him must have been a serious occupational hazard of the early analysts. A decade earlier another analyst, Viktor Tausk, who like Reich was a non-practising Jew from an outlying province of the Austro-Hungarian Empire, was refused an analysis by Freud. According to Paul Roazen's study of Tausk (New York, 1969) this rejection by Freud initiated a reaction which ended in Tausk's suicide six months later. Incidentally, a paper by Tausk also appears in Fliess's *Psychoanalytic Reader*.

Whatever the inner story of Reich's break with Freud and psychoanalysis may be, the following appears to be the correct chronology :

1927. Reich seeks analysis with Freud, who refuses to treat him. The first version[2] of Reich's *The Function of the Orgasm* is published by the International Psychoanalytic Publishing House. Reich spends some months in a Swiss sanatorium.

1928. Reich joins the Austrian Communist Party. With four other analysts and three obstetricians he founds the Socialist Society for Sex Consultation and Sexological Research.

1929. Reich visits Russia. His *Dialectical Materialism and Psychoanalysis* is published in Moscow.

1930. Reich moves to Berlin. He founds the German Association for Proletarian Sexual Politics, whose aims include the abolition of laws against abortion and homo-

---

2. 'Version', not 'edition'. Reich had the bibliographically maddening habit of completely rewriting books for their later editions, or to put it the other way round, of giving old titles to entirely new books.

sexuality and the dissemination of birth control information.

1933. Reich publishes *The Mass Psychology of Fascism* in
Denmark. He is expelled from the German Communist
Party. The first version of Reich's *Character Analysis* is
printed by the International Psychoanalytical Publishing
House, but without its imprint.

1934. Reich is expelled or rather 'dropped' or 'edged out'
of the International Psychoanalytical Association—the
details of this process are too complicated and obscure to
be worth elucidating.

In retrospect, neither of these two expulsions seems
intellectually justified, though in view of the political
circumstances of the time they are perhaps forgivable.
The psychoanalytical movement felt it had no chance of
surviving the rise of fascism if it was associated with
communism—the German Psychoanalytical Society
several times asked Reich to resign for this reason but he
always refused—while the Communist Party felt he was
diverting into mental and sexual hygiene campaigns
energies which were required for direct political action.
But in the event the psychoanalytical movement's hope
of riding the storm of fascism by claiming to be a pure
science and unpolitical proved illusory, and the defeat of
the communist and socialist movements by fascism can
hardly be laid at the door of Reich's diversions into
sexology. Nor in retrospect do the psychoanalytical
movement's objections to the first version of Reich's
Character Analysis seem justifiable or comprehensible
intellectually; almost all of it had already appeared previously in psychoanalytical journals and the decision to

withhold official blessing seems to have been based solely on grounds of political expediency.

From now on Reich was on his own. He was a member of no established organization and his ideas had been rejected by two movements to which he had given himself wholly. From now on too, anyone who attempts to follow the development of his ideas is in serious difficulties. Either he continues to take Reich seriously, in which case he runs the risk of being converted to a way of thinking which would put him, in Reich's own words, 'beyond the intellectual framework of present-day character structure and, with that, the civilization of the last 5,000 years', or he ceases to do so, in which case he runs the risk of falling into a methodological trap, that of using Reich's personality as an argument against his ideas. Even Reich's greatest admirers admit that he was a difficult and autocratic man and it is not hard to point to aspects of his life and writings which call his sanity into question—the two possible psychiatric diagnoses are hypomania for his early years and paranoia for his later—but there are, it seems to me, several objections to using this all too easy way out.

First, if Reich *was* right and he really did 'step beyond the intellectual framework of present-day character structure', diagnostic labels which derive from this intellectual framework are inapplicable to him—or indeed to anyone else. Society's views on who is sane and who is mad obviously depend to a large extent on its criteria of normality, and as a result anyone who questions its norms runs the risk of being considered mad. All prophets, world-shakers and dreamers of dreams are at risk in this way, and indeed a large number of them have been manhandled by psychiatrists and analysts foolish enough to rush in where angels fear to tread. Jesus Christ has been diagnosed schizophrenic, Beethoven paranoid, the Old Testament prophets (collectively) schizophrenoid, Leonardo da Vinci schizoid-obsessional, etc., etc. Although psychiatric excursions of this kind are not always without interest, they suffer from two grave limitations. They assume that contemporary psychoanalytical theory has achieved timeless objectivity, that the criteria by which we now assess human personality are independent of the historical processes that have led to the emergence of the Freudian conception of human nature; and they fail to escape from the reductionist tendencies built into psychoanalytical theories and therefore in effect if not in intention they tend to invalidate the ideas produced by the individuals subjected to this sort of treatment. It seems to me that no amount of study of the origins of new ideas in the minds of those who first formulated them help one to make the crucial decision, whether these ideas are true or false. Both true and false prophets must have had their infantile traumata, their Oedipus complexes and their neuroses.

Fortunately Reich made one claim for his ideas which simplifies matters enormously for anyone attempting to assess them. He claimed to have discovered not only the truth about the nature of energy and of love, but also that these truths were demonstrable by the techniques of the natural sciences. His truths were not poetic or religious or artistic truths but scientific truths which could, he claimed, be confirmed by anyone who repeated his experiments. Anyone who attempts to evaluate his ideas is therefore entitled to use as critical weapons the available evidence bearing on such questions as : (1) did Reich understand the nature of scientific method? (2) Did he have a good and thorough knowledge of biology and physics, the two sciences on which he leaned most heavily? (3) Did he construct his experiments with scientific rigour and with proper respect for the need for controls? (4) Have his ideas on physics and biology attracted sympathetic interest among those experts best qualified to understand and assess them? All these are legitimate questions since in one respect Reich certainly did not 'step beyond the intellectual framework of present-day human character structure'. Although he became increasingly interested in aspects of human nature which have traditionally been the domain of the humanities and even of religious mysticism, he retained throughout his life the belief that rationalism and the natural sciences are the only avenue to the truth.

Although, or so it seems to me, the answers to the four questions I posed above must be 'no', this does not, I believe, dispose of Reich. He might after all have been wrong in supposing that all truths are natural-scientific truths and yet have arrived at insights of value. Even if he was wrong in believing that the methods of natural science are appropriate for the study of human nature, some at least of his ideas might be valid, even if misplaced and ill-based. What I am suggesting here, and hope to substantiate later, is that Reich was barking up the wrong tree and that his allegiance to the natural sciences compelled him to deceive himself into believing that his ideas about energy, love and the cosmos were the result of his scientific researches when in fact they were the product of some inner process of development which led him to conclusions which a number of poets, mystics and theologians have reached by subjective and largely introspective routes. In so deceiving himself he developed to an absurdity a tendency which was also present in Freud, who consistently converted the insights into human nature which he gained through his self-analysis and from his professional association with neurotic patients into objective and impersonal sounding theories which were intended to satisfy the criteria of the natural sciences.

After this digression I must return to my summary account of Reich's life, though I must confess to a certain sense of unreality about doing so. This derives from two sources. First, Reich's career and ideas up to the mid-1930s are clearly related to time and place. His interest in psychoanalysis could only have developed and taken the form it did in Vienna in the 1920s; and it constitutes a contribution to an intellectual movement which began before he entered it and which continues into the present. Similarly his marxism and his political activities are inexplicable without references to the social tragedy by which he and all those close to him were overwhelmed. But after 1934 his ideas take a private course; he has followers who accept his ideas, usually after having been his patients, but no external influences seem to work on him, and as a result it seems irrelevant to know which of his ideas and therapeutic innovations date from his stay in Denmark, which first saw the light of day during the two years he spent in Norway, and which date from after 1938 when he settled in the U.S.A. It is however important to know that in the U.S.A. his therapeutic practice was successful enough to provide him with funds to conduct his researches on an extensive scale, to found journals and to set up a foundation for the propagation of his ideas and a Wilhelm Reich Infant Trust Fund for their advancement after his death.

Finally, I must mention his trial and death in prison, since these are events which play an important part in the mythology which surrounds Reich. By the 1950s Reich had persuaded himself that it was possible to isolate life energy in the form of vesicles, which he called bions, and to store it in accumulators known as orgone boxes. He also believed that it was possible to cure patients with cancer and other diseases by placing them inside these boxes. In 1954 the United States Food and Drug Administration placed an injunction against the distribution of orgone boxes on the ground that the claims made on their behalf were fraudulent. Reich refused both to obey the injunction and to recognize the competence of the courts to adjudicate on matters of scientific fact. He was eventually charged with contempt of court and sentenced to two years' imprisonment. After imprisonment he was diagnosed paranoid and transferred to 'Lewisburg, which was the only penitentiary with psychiatric treatment facilities', where he was however declared 'legally sane and competent'. On November 3rd, 1957, he died of a heart disease.

2 Energy, Character and Orgasm

Reich's ideas about energy, character and orgasm can only be understood in the light of their origin in the kind of psychoanalysis which he encountered in Vienna in the 1920s. At that time psychoanalysis was still under the unquestioned influence of Freud's ideal of a psychological theory which would satisfy all the criteria of a natural science.

As a young man Freud had worked as a physiologist under Ernst Brücke, who was a leading member of a crusading anti-vitalist, scientific movement usually known as the Helmholtz School of Medicine. The aims of this school are epitomized by a 'solemn oath' pledged in 1842 by Brücke and his fellow psychologist Du Bois-Reymond:

> No other forces than the common physical and chemical ones are active within the organism. In those cases which cannot at present be explained by these forces one either has to find the specific way or form of their action by means of the physical–mathematical method or to assume new forces equal in dignity to the chemical–physical forces inherent in matter, reducible to the force of attraction and repulsion . . .

The Helmholtz school was reductionist and both anti-idealist and anti-religious. It was concerned to ensure that religious and vitalist concepts such as 'spirit', 'élan vital', 'life force' were excluded from the biological

sciences and to demonstrate that the structure and behaviour of living organisms were explicable solely in
terms of the concepts of physics and chemistry. Their
standpoint was strictly determinist and assumed that all
explanations are in terms of causation; they seem to
have been strangely untroubled by the possibility that
the emergence of consciousness, and in man of reflective
self-awareness, might pose awkward problems when it
came to applying causal-deterministic modes of thought
to the behaviour of man and the higher animals.

Inspired by this ideal, Freud's lifelong ambition was to
construct a scientific psychology in which mental phenomena could be shown to be subject to the laws of
causation and to be reducible to a number of simple
statements about the forces of attraction and repulsion
operating within a system or structure consisting of
mental units or 'ideas'. He assumed that there exists
some form of mental energy 'which possesses all the
characteristics of quantity (though we have no means of
measuring it), which is capable of increase, diminution,
displacement and discharge, and which is spread over
the memory traces of ideas somewhat as an electric
charge is spread over the surface of a body.'[1] He assumed further that this mental energy circulated within
a Mental Apparatus, which was conceived to have structure. In Freud's original formulations this structure consisted of a Conscious and an Unconscious, but in 1923,
with the publication of Freud's The Ego and the Id, the
mental apparatus became tripartite, consisting of an Id,
and Ego and a Super-ego. Ideas, impulses, emotions, etc.,
were conceived to be located at specific points in this
apparatus; changes in feeling, desire and thought were

1. Freud, S. (1894). 'The Neuro-Psychoses of Defence', in
Standard Edition, Vol. III. London 1962.

explained as the result of movements of quanta of energy from one part of the mental apparatus to another, while actions were conceived to be accompanied by discharge of energy.

Despite the fact that Freud's 'scientific psychology' is patently a form of science fiction, with its quanta of unquantifiable energy and its transposition of temporal relationships into spatial ones (in the mental apparatus, the past is underneath the present and ideas move upwards as they become conscious), in Freud's own writings it sounds very scientific and objective and Freud's followers in the 1920s seem, with the possible exceptions of Lou Andreas-Salomé and Oscar Pfister, to have been entirely oblivious of the complications produced by the fact that the data which it purported to explain were subjective phenomena, derived from introspection and reminiscence. They seem to have accepted without question Freud's assumption that the translation of human experience into the language of the natural sciences was a worthwhile activity, and not, as many contemporary analysts now believe, an unprofitable if sometimes amusing game.

Since Reich's later researches were primarily concerned with the nature of biological energy, two of Freud's ideas about mental energy must be mentioned briefly. First, he held that it existed in two forms, one mobile and the other 'bound', mobile energy being characteristic of unconscious mental processes, which were regarded as 'chaotic' and unstructured, bound energy being characteristic of conscious mental processes, which were regarded as having structure and organization. Since Freud also held that mental energy has its origin in bodily processes, this idea that mind consists of energy existing in two forms bears a remarkable resemblance to William Blake's statement that 'Energy is the only life and is from the body; and reason is the bound and outward circumference of energy'.

Secondly, he usually, though not quite always, equated general mental energy and erotic energy, 'libido'. Here again his thinking is curiously similar to Blake's 'Energy is eternal delight'. However, despite the similarities between Freud's and Blake's views on the nature of mental energy, they differ fundamentally in respect of their origins and credentials. Blake reached his insight by an admitted act of poetic imagination, while Freud claimed to have reached his by scientific observation and reasoning.

Although Freud's first theories about mental energy and structure, which are described in his *Project for a Scientific Psychology*, written in 1895 but only published posthumously, were formulated in the hope that they would prove to correspond precisely with the way the brain works, he later saw clearly that his Mental Apparatus was a fiction, a metaphorical system which did not necessarily bear any real relation to the physiological and neurological processes accompanying and underlying mental activity. However, like all analogies, it could and often was taken literally by the philosophically unwary, and I think that there can be little doubt that Reich believed in the objective reality of Freud's Mental Apparatus.

However, despite his acceptance of the mechanist assumptions underlying the idea of the Mental Apparatus, Reich was also a vitalist, both by temperament and conviction. In the early 1920s he read a lot of Bergson, acquiring indeed the reputation of being a 'crazy Bergsonian', and in the biographical chapter of the 1942 version of *The Function of the Orgasm* there is a revealing passage which shows that he always wanted to replace ideas by things and to resolve the vitalist–mechanist antithesis by discovering some *thing* in which the life force could be located.

'For some time, I was taken for a "crazy Bergsonian", because I agreed with him in principle, without, however, being able to state exactly where his theory left a gap. His *élan vital* was highly reminiscent of Driesch's "entelechy". There was no denying the principle of creative power governing life; only it was not satisfactory as long as it was not tangible, as long as it could not be described or practically handled. For, rightly, this was considered the supreme goal of natural science. The vitalists seemed to come closer to an understanding of the life principle than the mechanists who dissected life before trying to understand it. On the other hand, the concept of the organism working like a machine was more appealing to the intellect; one could think in terms of what one had learned from physics' (pp. 6–7).

As we shall see, Reich eventually persuaded himself that he had succeeded in reconciling the vitalist 'understanding of the life principle' with the mechanist appeal to the intellect by discovering a substance, which could be touched and 'practically handled', in which the life force was embodied.

Just as Reich's ideas on life-energy derive from Freud's ideas on mental energy and libido, so too his ideas on 'character' can be traced back to Freud's concept of 'defence'.

According to Freud, unconscious ideas and wishes do not just happen to be unconscious. On the contrary, they strive energetically to become conscious but are prevented from becoming so by the action of 'defence mechanisms', the best known and first described of these mechanisms being repression. In other words the mind, the mental apparatus, is assumed to be divided into two parts, an instinctual part which strives for self-expression and for recurrent discharge of its accumulating energies, and another 'reasonable' part which is concerned to maintain its equilibrium and to avoid tension, stress and anxiety. If the wishes of the former part, the id, are felt to threaten the latter part's equilibrium or to endanger its relation to the outside world (by instigating actions which will be met by frustration, opposition or social and moral disapproval), this latter part, the ego, will attempt to protect itself from the anticipated distress and to ensure itself against disappointment and disapproval by activating defences which prevent the disturbing impulse from becoming conscious.

There is, it will be noted, something ambiguous about this conception of the mind as a structure inherently divided against itself. The equilibrium-seeking part, the ego, is conceived to suffer from divided loyalties. On the one hand, it wishes to experience the joys and pleasures of self-expression, of 'instinctual satisfaction'; on the other hand, it seeks to accommodate itself to the limitations of the environment it finds itself in and to the moral values of the society of which it is a member. Moreover, since the ego is held to internalize (or identify with) these moral values, and to construct within itself a third structure, the super-ego, whose inner commands it feels impelled to obey, the unfortunate ego is conceived to have the unenviable task of trying to reconcile three often incompatible sets of demands, those of the id, those of the super-ego and those of the environment.

Now, although this theory purports to be scientific

and morally neutral, and although too it can be used to describe and classify neurotic states in terms of such concepts as 'the strength of the instincts', 'the severity of the super-ego', 'the strength of the ego', etc., the practical conclusions drawn from it are likely to depend to a considerable extent on the personality and temperament of the person using it. If he is an optimist who holds that man is basically good and sets a high value of self-expressive activity, he is likely to be pro-id and will tend to regard the super-ego and social morality as the villains of the piece; while if he is a pessimist convinced of man's evil and destructiveness, he will tend to side with the ego's struggle to master and control its unruly instinctual endowment.

It would be convenient and dramatically satisfying if it were possible to maintain that Freud was basically a pessimist opposed to the instincts and Reich an optimist wholeheartedly on the side of instinctual self-expression. This opposition is indeed sometimes assumed by Reich's followers, but it is, I think, unfair to both Freud and Reich.

Freud did, it is true, sometimes write very negatively about the id, which he once described as a 'cauldron of seething excitations', while in his *Civilization and Its Discontents* he developed the thesis that the development of all culture and civilization is unavoidably based on instinctual renunciation. However, he seems also to have held that instinctual renunciation involves a real and regrettable loss—i.e. his theory of culture is ironical and tragic and not ascetic—and in his paper 'Civilized Sexual Morality and Modern Nervousness' he states unequivocally his conviction that our own (or rather his, since this paper was written in 1908) civilization demands more renunciation of its members than is necessary for its preservation. As Ernest Jones[2] says of this paper, 'it was in essence a protest against the exorbitant demands of society, especially in the sexual sphere, on the life of the individual. The grounds of this protest are as valid now as then, but in some respects the paper has an interest as a period piece. It depicts a civilization in many ways different from our present one, and it can be said that some of the important changes in the past half-century are the direct result of Freud's own work.'[3]

Nor, although Reich certainly was an optimist who believed that inside every corrupted, civilized man there was a Rousseauan Noble Savage trying to escape, is it true that he believed in instinctual freedom in the sense of supposing that each and every desire should be acted upon immediately. Although he held that sexual deprivation produces states of 'sexual stasis' which provided the energy with which neuroses are engendered and perpetuated, his conceptions of sexual potency and

2. Ernest Jones, *Sigmund Freud, Life and Work*, vol. ii, p. 328. London 1955.

3. The idea that civilization is based on instinctual renunciation was a conclusion that seemed to follow inevitably from Freud's theory of sublimation, but I doubt whether many contemporary analysts subscribe to it. According to Freud's theory of sublimation, all 'higher' mental functions evolve out of 'lower' physical ones, use energy which in the first instance belongs to these lower ones, and only develop insofar as the channels of expression of the lower, physical functions are blocked by frustration and repression. Modern psychoanalysis has extricated itself from the impasse created by this theory by postulating that the ego, in which higher mental functions are conceived to be located, has its own sources of energy independent of the id, and that 'sublimations' are inbuilt tendencies which emerge spontaneously under favourable conditions, although experiences of 'delay in satisfaction' are perhaps necessary for their development. See Heinz Hartmann's *The Ego and the Problem of Adaptation* (London 1958).

satisfaction included the necessity of total involvement of the personality in sexual relationships. He also maintained that the truly healthy man, the so-called 'genital character', possessed a natural internal regulating function which makes socially enforced 'compulsive morality' unnecessary.

'The healthy individual has no compulsive morality because he has no impulses which call for moral inhibition ... Intercourse with a prostitute becomes impossible. Sadistic phantasies disappear. To expect love as a right or even to rape the sexual partner becomes inconceivable, as do ideas of seducing children. Anal, exhibitionistic or other perversions disappear, and with these the social anxiety and guilt feelings. The incestuous fixation to parents and siblings loses its interest; this liberates the energy which was bound up in such fixations. In brief, all these phenomena point to the fact that the organism is capable of *self-regulation*' (*The Sexual Revolution*, pp. 6–7).

In this connection it is amusing to note that in one passage in the Function of the Orgasm Reich expresses with such definiteness his conviction that 'genital characters' are moral that his American translator found it necessary to insert a footnote designed to reassure readers that Reich did not believe in life-long monogamy, but only that sexual relationships, while they last, constitute a bond to which neither partner wishes to be unfaithful.

'The idea of a natural (as distinct from a compulsive) morality is so alien to most people that in talking or writing about it one is always in danger of being misunderstood. In going over the manuscript, Dr Silverberg pointed out a possible misunderstanding at this point; with his permission I am quoting his comment: "I would suggest some emendation here in order to avert the impression that orgasmotherapy makes people monogamous. As I gather the meaning, the orgastically potent woman takes her sexual life seriously enough not to want to fritter her energies away indiscriminately, but is apt to let each relationship develop and run its own course, one at a time. This does not mean that she remains 'true' to one man all her life, but only so long as the relationship with him 'lasts', a period determined by certain inner laws within the relationship itself and usually of considerably longer duration than is implied in the case of the woman who sleeps with every Tom, Dick and Harry. I think Dr Reich should make it clear that he is not referring here to 'monogamy' in its present-day usage of 'true to one man until death (or divorce) do us part'." This comment makes the point quite clear.' (Translator's note: *The Function of the Orgasm*, p. 152.)

Freud's idea that the ego defends itself against impulses arising in the id leads naturally to the idea that a person's 'character' may be a defence, and to the clinical concept that in addition to psychoneurotics whose symptoms are the result of conflict between repressed and repressing aspects of their personality, there are also 'character-neurotics' whose habitual stances and attitudes are interpretable as defences against unwelcome, unconscious instinctual tendencies. In such people character-traits are the equivalents of symptoms, since they are compulsive, involuntary patterns of behaviour whose function it is to prevent the emergence of repressed impulses. Examples of such character-defences are habitual submissiveness and obsequiousness preventing the emergence of envy and hostility, habitual solicitousness covering cruelty and habitual assertiveness acting as a defence against unconscious wishes to be passive and dependent.

This idea that a person's 'character', in the sense of his habitual, stereotyped attitudes and responses to situations, is a defence has become an essential part of every analyst's intellectual equipment, but Reich cannot be credited with it, since it can be traced back in the psychoanalytical literature at least as far as 1908, when Freud published his 'Character and Anal Erotism'. He does, however, seem to have been the first analyst to appreciate that it might be possible and indeed necessary to treat patients by interpreting the nature and functions of their character rather than by analysing their dreams and free associations. Even when he was a conventional analyst he took the view that it was a waste of time listening to a patient's free associations or interpreting his dreams unless the analyst had previously made him aware of his habitual attitude of, say, submissiveness or rudeness towards the analyst and had succeeded in getting him to understand why he found it necessary to relate to him in such a stereotyped way. Only after this had been made clear to the patient could the patient, in Reich's view, become at ease and spontaneous with his analyst and open up sincerely to him in a way that made his free associations valid communications.

Reich's advocacy of character-analysis in addition or in preference to symptom-analysis and dream-interpretation also contributed to the realization that the therapeutic effect of psychotherapy derives not from the unearthing of traumatic memories or from the correct interpretation of dreams and symptoms but from the nature of the relationship which develops between analyst and patient. By insisting on the importance of analysing the patient's defences against allowing spontaneous rapport to develop between himself and the analyst, he opened up the possibility of discovering what really goes on between them and contributed significantly to the idea that psychotherapy consists in a confrontation or encounter between two real, live people. As a result his work constitutes a formative, though not always acknowledged influence, not only on contemporary psychoanalysis with its emphasis on the importance of transference and counter-transference interactions, but also on the existentialist, contractual and 'encounter' schools of psychotherapy. (See particularly the writings of R. D. Laing, Rollo May, Alexander Lowen and F. S Perls.)

However, Reich was not content to stop here. He soon went further, maintaining that character was *the* essential defence in *all* cases and that civilized western man was imprisoned in a character-armour, which prevented him, in general, from expressing his spontaneous feelings of love and hatred, and in particular from experiencing orgasm. This character-armour represented the precipitation within his personality of society's anti-emotional, anti-libidinal 'compulsive morality', the origins of which Reich explained in terms of his social and political theories. These are discussed later in Chapter 3.

Reich's theory of orgasm also has its roots in Freud's thinking. According to Freud (1894) the neuroses could be divided into two groups, actual neuroses and psychoneuroses; the former being the direct, physiological result of present-day (*aktuel*) disturbances of sexual function, the latter being complicated, psychological consequences of past experiences. Actual neuroses, being of physiological origin, were incapable of psychological interpretation and did not require it; they were cured automatically if the patient abandoned unhealthy sexual habits such as excessive masturbation, coitus interruptus or abstinence. On the other hand the psychoneuroses, being complex psychological formations, could only be explained and cured by psychoanalytical investigation and interpretation of the patient's Odeipus complex and infantile sexual phantasies and by the recovery of repressed, traumatic experiences.

Although this distinction between actual and psychoneuroses was in theory simple and straightforward, in practice matters were more complicated. If one sought to explain why any particular patient allowed himself to develop an actual neurosis, it often became necessary to postulate the simultaneous presence of a psychoneurosis which prevented him from organizing for himself a satisfactory sex-life; while, since psychoneuroses lead to sexual inhibitions, they were bound to be compounded by a super-imposed actual neurosis.

As a result some analysts denied the usefulness of the distinction, while even more denied the existence of the actual neuroses and sought to explain all neuroses and all neurotic anxiety in purely psychological terms. Reich, however, took the opposite stance, maintaining that an actual neurosis formed the core of every psychoneurosis. 'The psychoneurosis had an actual–neurotic core and the actual neuroses had a psychoneurotic superstructure' (*The Function of the Orgasm*, p. 69). Furthermore he argued that it was the inability of psychoneurotics to discharge sexual energy completely and with satisfaction during orgasm which created the damming up of energy (the 'sexual stasis' in his terminology) which kept the psychoneurosis alive. In other words he thought that neurotics were caught in a vicious circle. Their actual neurosis provided the energy to create and maintain their psychoneurosis which then perpetuated their actual neurosis.

This view of the relationship between actual and psychoneuroses has not been absorbed into psychoanalytical thinking, but it has two great merits. It retains a connection between psychopathology and physiology—in the last resort the neuroses are not purely mental formations but arise from and affect the body—and it provides an explanation of why neuroses do not recover spontaneously. So far as I know Reich is the only analyst to offer any sort of explanation as to why the childhood pathogenic experiences which according to psychoanalysis cause neuroses do not gradually lose their impact when neurotics move away from their childhood environment.

Now, since, as Reich himself readily admitted, many psycho-neurotics appeared or claimed to be living normal and satisfactory sex lives, his position compelled him to call into question the normality and authenticity of much that passes for normal sex. In particular, he challenged the idea that orgastic potency could be defined simply in terms of the capacity for erection, penetration and ejaculation (and *mutatis mutandis* for women). These capacities were, he maintained, only 'the indispensable prerequisites for orgastic potency'. True orgastic potency included these but both involved much more and excluded much that passed for normal. It involved, *inter alia*, 'the capacity for surrender to the flow of biological energy without any inhibition, the capacity for complete discharge of all dammed-up sexual excitation through involuntary pleasurable contractions of the body' (not just of the genitals). It excluded the presence of any trace of sadism in the male or masochism in the female, or any sense of prowess or smugness in the male.

Furthermore, the surrender is silent or nearly so. Orgastically potent individuals never talk or laugh during the sexual act—with the exception of uttering words of tenderness. Both talking and laughing indicate a serious lack of the capacity for surrender, which requires an undivided absorption in the sensations of pleasure. Men to whom surrender means being 'feminine' are always orgastically 'disturbed'.

With such high criteria in mind Reich was surely right in asserting that 'not a single neurotic individual possesses orgastic potency; the corollary of this fact is the fact that the vast majority of humans suffer from a character-neurosis'. His theories of character-armour and orgasm constitute therefore a sweeping indictment of the sexual life of civilized man, an indictment similar in many ways to that made by D. H. Lawrence, who indeed he resembled in combining an intense almost mystical belief in the prime importance of sex with a puritanical insistence that it should always be treated with high if not dead seriousness. He and Lawrence also had in common the conviction that orgastic potency is a virtue to be found more commonly among working class men than among aristocrats, bourgeois and intellectuals, an idea for which no evidence exists. 'There are human beings of a certain kind, living and working here and there, unobtrusively, who are equipped with *natural* sexuality; they are the *genital characters*. They are found frequently among the industrial workers' (*The Function of the Orgasm*, p. 171).

In working out his theory of the function of the orgasm in preserving and maintaining health, Reich was led to make a minute analysis of the 'orgastically satisfying sexual act'. This is described, complete with a graph, in Chapter iv, Section 3 of the 1942 version of *The*

Function of the Orgasm—which was written after he had persuaded himself that libido (bio-energy) is a 'tangible' substance whose movements in the body can be traced and recorded electrically.

Reich's account of the ideal sexual act is remarkable both for its explicitness, which must have required courage in the pre-Kinsey, pre-Masters and Johnson era in which it was written, and for its omission of the word 'love'. And yet it is clear that it is love that he is talking about. Orgastic potency as formulated by Reich is the capacity to love body and soul, psychosomatically.

Another remarkable feature of this account of the sexual act is Reich's insistence that in genital characters it differs physically as well as psychologically from that experienced by the orgastically immature. Whereas the typical, civilized man with his inhibiting character-armour only experiences 'partial releases of tension which are *similar* to orgasm', the genital character experiences an 'ultimate vegetatively involuntary surrender' of which lesser mortals have no inkling. Even if one succeeds in attaching some meaning to this phrase and is prepared to accept the idea that there may exist people, presumably either untreated industrial workers or ex-patients of Reich's, who are familiar with this ultimate vegetatively involuntary surrender, one is still left wondering how Reich knew, from what experiences of his own or his patients he derived this insight—or even more how he reached by natural–scientific means the conclusion that 'all feelings about nature derive from this function or from the longing for it'.

Reich's conviction that all neurotics and indeed most civilized men and women lack full orgastic potency, coupled with his belief in the existence of sexual energies requiring recurrent orgastic discharge, raised for him the question of what happened to these energies when they were not effectively discharged. One answer was, as already mentioned, that they were expended in neurotic symptoms and systems of thought and provided the energy which activated and maintained infantile sexual phantasies. Another answer was that they were experienced as anxiety. Undischarged energy, which would have been experienced as pleasure if it had been discharged orgastically, is experienced as anxiety if it is discharged through other bodily systems. Here again Reich was following a line of thought begun by Freud, whose original theory of anxiety was that undischarged libido is 'converted' into anxiety. This theory, which Freud himself abandoned in the nineteen-twenties, assumed that anxiety is a direct physiological result of repressed sexual tension, but the precise nature of the process designated 'conversion' was admitted to be mysterious. Reich, in line with his general tendency to remain loyal to Freud's early ideas and to reject his later reformulations, sought to retain Freud's idea of the intimate, physiological connection between libido and anxiety by solving the mystery of conversion. This he did by maintaining that anxiety is simply libidinal discharge occurring through the cardiovascular system. Whereas sexual pleasure is experienced in the genitals, anxiety is experienced in the cardiac and diaphragmatic region: 'Freud's original formulation thus underwent the following correction. *There is no conversion* of sexual excitation into anxiety. *The same excitation which appears in the genital as pleasure, manifests itself as anxiety if it stimulates the cardiovascular system.* That is, in the latter case it appears as the *exact opposite of pleasure.* ... sexuality and anxiety present two opposite directions of vegetative excitation' (*The Function of the*

Orgasm, p. 110).

Reich's third answer to the question of the fate of undischarged libido was that it was transformed into sadism; the repressed wish for true orgasm continues to strive for discharge and the resulting aggression, which in healthy persons is only a means to an end, 'becomes itself the behaviour which will release tension. Aggression then becomes pleasurable *as such*. In this way, sadism arises. The loss of the real love aim results in hatred. One hates most when one is prevented from loving or being loved. Thus, aggression assumes the character of destructiveness *with sexual aims*, as, e.g. in sex murder. Its prerequisite is the complete inability to experience sexual pleasure in a natural way. The perversion 'sadism' (the impulse to satisfy oneself by hurting or destroying the object) is, therefore, a mixture of primary sexual and secondary destructive impulses. It does not exist in the animal kingdom and is a recent acquisition of man, *a secondary drive*. Every kind of *destructive action by itself is the reaction of the organism to the denial of the gratification of a vital need, especially the sexual*' (*The Function of the Orgasm*, p. 132).

And two paragraphs later: 'I made inquiries about the behaviour of wild animals and learned that they are harmless when their hunger and their sexual needs are satisfied. Bulls are only dangerous when being led to the cow, not on being led away. Dogs are dangerous when kept on the chain, because exercise and sexual satisfaction are made impossible. The cruel character traits of people with chronic lack of sexual satisfaction thus became understandable. They are well-known, e.g. in sharp-tongued spinsters and ascetic moralists. The mildness and kindness of individuals capable of genital satisfaction was striking in contrast. I have never seen individuals capable of genital satisfaction who had sadistic character traits. If such people showed sadistic tendencies, it could safely be assumed that they had met with a sudden obstacle to their accustomed gratification ...'

I have quoted Reich's views on sadism extensively since they form the basis and rationale for the contemporary slogan Make Love Not War. This injunction contains Reich in a nutshell. It appeals immediately to all that is warm, generous and spontaneous in human nature. It assumes an extraordinarily direct and simple connection between orgastic deprivation and destructiveness—according to Reich even genital characters become sadists if confronted with a sudden obstacle to their accustomed gratification. And yet it is naive by its omissions. Just as Reich's confident assertions about the natural placidity and peacefulness of bulls and dogs completely ignore the aggressiveness associated with territoriality (see the writings of Lorenz, Storr and Ardrey) and the establishment of hierarchical 'pecking orders' within animal communities, so the Make Love Not War philosophy completely ignores the psychology of power —and in practical terms such complications as the fact that those who decide to make wars are not under modern conditions the people who fight in them and that there is no evidence that the majority of those who do do the fighting get any sadistic gratification out of doing so.

Finally, it must be emphasized that all Reich's ideas about the effects of orgastic frustration derive from psychoanalytical ways of thinking, and were in his own view a defence of Freud's original position against a retrogressive development in psychoanalysis emanating from Freud himself. In the mid 1920s both Freud and Reich, presumably for the same social and historical reasons, became impressed by man's tendency to behave destructively, but whereas Freud sought to explain this by postulating a Death Instinct, an innate drive towards destructiveness and self-destruction, Reich adopted the explanation that it was due to a much greater and more widespread repression of sexuality than Freud had ever envisaged. And in taking up this position Reich conceived himself to be defending Freud's original revolutionary insights against a loss of nerve and hope on Freud's part.

Both explanations, however, raised as many problems as they solved. Freud's raised problems about the evolutionary status of an instinct that appeared to run counter to evolution, while Reich's raised problems about the origin of man's tendency to construct a character-armour against his own nature. Freud's biological justification of the death instinct concept is singularly unconvincing, since, as Jones, a loyal Freudian if ever there was one, says 'No biological observation can be found to support the idea of a death instinct, one which contradicts all biological principles', and it has been accepted by only a minority even of psychoanalysts. It has however contributed to the widespread belief that psychoanalysis is the modern dismal science which sets limits on human progress. Reich, as we shall see, produced at different phases of his life two different and incompatible explanations of the origin of the tendency to construct character-armour, the first sociological and the second 'religious'. Both are still with us; the second indeed always has been, since it resembles closely the account of the Fall of Man given in Genesis.

3   Reich and the Sexual Paradise

Reich's conviction of the prime importance of orgasm in maintaining health, both mental and physical, and in preventing neurosis, led him to formulate a theory of sex-economy, which contains within itself both a theory of psychopathology and a critique of capitalist society. These are, however, incomprehensible unless one realizes that for Reich the concept of orgasm embraced all that is joyous and spontaneous. His conviction was, if I understand him rightly, that life could be freer and more untrammelled than civilized societies allow it to be, and that if man could live by his instincts and not in submission to his character-armour, life would not only be freer and richer than it is but also that many moral problems and indeed many physical illnesses including cancer would never occur. He seems indeed to have believed that suffering is in principle unnecessary, an artefact produced by social restrictions imposed on the life and the wisdom of the body. It is characteristic of his approach that his writings never touch on such awkward problems for the utopian as the inevitability of ageing or man's awareness of his mortality. As a result his philosophy of life contained no place for the need for consolation which so many religions claim to supply, nor for the search for meaning. Orgasm and other spontaneous activities were in Reich's view good and meaningful in themselves, and required neither justification nor explanation. Nor, until quite late in his life, does he appear to have considered the possibility that man's self-awareness and capacity to reflect upon his nature and destiny might inherently impair or even modify his capacity for direct animal, childlike enjoyment of living. It is not surprising that from early on in his career he refused to accept theological students and clergymen as patients.

However, Reich, despite his utopian vision of an orgastic, pre-lapsarian paradise, was also a practical man and his writings, particularly his *The Function of the Orgasm* and *The Sexual Revolution* contain specific recommendations for reforms which would increase the incidence of sexual happiness and reduce that of neurosis.

These reforms are derived and justified by Reich from his theory of sex-economy, which constitutes the core of his thinking. Since, as I know from personal experience, Reich's present followers are all too ready to accuse anyone who writes about him of at the least misrepresenting him and at the worst of vilifying him, I shall present this central part of Reich's thinking by extensive quotation from his introduction to the 1942 version of *The Function of the Orgasm*, where he affirms that 'the theory of sex-economy can be put in a few sentences'. In fact it takes him three pages (xviii–xx). In the following numbered paragraphs I quote the main points of his argument.

1. 'Psychic health depends on orgastic potency, that is, on the capacity for surrender in the acme of sexual excitation in the natural act. Its basis is the un-neurotic character attitude of capacity for love.'

2. 'Mental illness is a result of a disturbance in the natural capacity for love. In the case of orgastic impotence, from which a vast majority of humans are suffer-

39

ing, biological energy is dammed up, thus becoming the source of all kinds of irrational behaviour.'

3. 'Psychic disturbances are the results of the sexual chaos brought about by the nature of our society. This chaos has, for thousands of years, served the function of making people submissive to existing conditions, in other words, of internalizing the external mechanization of life. It serves the purpose of bringing about the *psychic anchoring* of a mechanized and authoritarian civilization by way of making people lack self-confidence.'

4. 'The vital energies, under natural conditions, regulate themselves spontaneously, without compulsive duty or compulsive morality.'

5. 'Antisocial behavior springs from secondary drives which owe their existence to the suppression of natural sexuality.'

6. 'The individual brought up in an atmosphere which negates life and sex acquires a pleasure-anxiety (fear of pleasurable excitation) which is represented physiologically in chronic muscular spasms. This pleasure-anxiety is the soil on which the individual re-creates the life-negating ideologies which are the basis of dictatorships. It is the foundation of the fear of a free, independent way of living.'

7. 'The character structure of man today—who is perpetuating a patriarchal, authoritarian culture some four to six thousands years old—is characterized by *an armouring against nature within himself and against social misery outside himself*. This armouring of the character is the basis of loneliness, helplessness, craving for authority, fear of responsibility, mystical longing, sexual misery, of impotent rebelliousness as well as of resignation of an unnatural and pathological type. Human beings have taken a hostile attitude toward that

in themselves which is living, and have alienated themselves from it. This alienation is not of biological, but of social and economic origin. It is not found in human history before the development of the patriarchal social order.'

8. 'Since then, duty has taken the place of the natural enjoyment of work and activity.'

9. 'This formation of character in the authoritarian mold has as its central point, not parental love, but *the authoritarian family*. Its chief instrument is the suppression of sexuality in the infant and the adolescent.'

10. 'Owing to the split in the human structure of to-day, nature and culture, instinct and morality, sexuality and achievement, are considered incompatible. That unity of culture and nature, work and love, morality and sexuality for which mankind is forever longing, this unity will remain a dream as long as man does not permit the satisfaction of the biological demands of natural (orgastic) sexual gratification.'

Although Reich's translators must presumably be held responsible for the shaky grammar and the erratic punctuation, this passage illustrates vividly two stylistic peculiarities of his writing, his repetitiveness and his inability to state precisely what he means. In sentences such as 'This formation of character in the authoritarian mold has as its central point, not parental love, but the authoritarian family', the general drift of his argument is clear— he is asserting that a particular 'authoritarian' mode of behaviour on the part of parents tends to produce a particular submissive, inhibited kind of character in their children—but his way of saying this is impressionistic and imprecise; it doesn't really make sense to say that a family can be a central point of a formation of character.

Reich's repetitiveness is, I think, a manifestation of a curious hectoring quality in his character which must have antagonized those who were not hypnotized by it. I, Wilhelm Reich, he seems to be saying, know the truth; and you, reader, have got to believe me and I'm going to go on telling you until you do. This note of strident, dogmatic assertiveness is unfortunately, but surely not accidentally, most apparent in his political writings when he is attacking fascism.

However, despite the repetitiveness and imprecision of Reich's own account, his theory of sex-economy is in fact capable of perfectly rational formulation. It is a theory which could be true, even if in fact it happens not to be. It can, I think, be summarized in seven propositions.

1. Mental health is dependent on the capacity to experience orgasm in Reich's psychosomatic meaning of the term.

2. Mental illness is the result of inhibition of the capacity to experience orgasm.

3. Inhibition of orgastic capacity is instituted and maintained by a defensive, psychological structure, character-armour.

4. Character-armour is represented physiologically by muscular tension and disturbances of posture.

5. Character-armour develops within the individual in response to external pressures antagonistic to sexual expression.

6. These anti-sexual pressures arise within a specific form of family, the 'authoritarian family', which is held together not by parental love, but by the oppressive and

repressive use of power by the father.

7. This form of family only occurs in patriarchal societies and is one of the techniques devised by such societies to produce a submissive population incapable of rebelling against its rulers.

1. The first of these propositions, that, in Reich's own words, 'psychic health depends on orgastic potency', is presented by him as a clinical fact, deriving its authority from the psychoanalytical observations of himself and other analysts. It is, however, open to two methodological objections; that it is tautological, and that it is formulated in a way that makes it impossible to say which comes first, the egg of orgastic potency or the chicken of mental health.

It is, of course, possible to define mental health in a way that designates as ill all persons who lack orgastic potency, and since Freud there has undoubtedly been a widespread tendency to do so, but such a procedure really begs the question, which is after all whether it is indeed a fact that all persons who feel well and whole— and who impress others as being so—possess orgastic potency, and that all persons who suffer mentally and seek psychiatric aid, lack it. Anyone who asserts, as Reich did, an exact correlation between health and orgastic capacity is under an obligation to demonstrate both that all apparently well-adjusted, healthy celibates prove on close investigation to be ill in some definable sense and that the orgastic capacity claimed for instance by some schizophrenics and manics is spurious. Reich fails to produce evidence bearing on either point.

Reich's assertion that mental health 'depends' on orgastic capacity also begs the question. Even if one agrees that there is some connection between the two, it by no means follows that the former depends on the latter. There are, after all, two other possibilities, that orgastic capacity depends on mental health, and that both are dependent on something else. This latter is, indeed, what Reich the scientist, as opposed to Reich the apostle of the orgasm, really thought. He held that there are two necessary preconditions for the development and maintenance of both mental health and orgastic potency; a childhood spent in a family in which infantile sexuality is not suppressed, and an adulthood spent in a society in which sexual activity is not restricted by religious taboos or economic restraints.

2. The second proposition that, again in Reich's own words, 'mental illness is a result of a disturbance in the natural capacity for love' is quite simply untrue. Although some mental illnesses, notably the psycho-neuroses and the sexual perversions, have arguably and indeed probably some connection with disturbances in the natural capacity for love, others quite certainly haven't. It is characteristic of Reich's utopianism and predilection for sweeping generalizations that he discusses mental illness as though he had never heard of mental deficiency or of organic mental illnesses caused by brain damage, metabolic disorders, senility, heredity, etc. And yet as a doctor and psychiatrist he must have been familiar with these illnesses, and have known that there is no way in which even the most ingenious intellect could make out a case for their being even remote results of a disturbance in the natural capacity for love.

3. In view of my earlier account of character-armour and its relation to the psychoanalytical concept of 'defence', it is unnecessary for me to discuss it further here, except perhaps to add that one of the problems created

by the idea of a ubiquitous character-armour imprisoning civilized man, is that of deciding which aspects of human culture are manifestations of the armour and which are expressions of forces within the natural man which succeed in surviving or transcending the armour. It is clear that in Reich's view all actions based on a sense of duty stem from the armour and that all actions based on a sense of compassion stem from the natural man, but much less clear to what extent he would have agreed with Marcuse, another post-Freudian marxist utopian, that much of bourgeois culture is 'affirmative', in the sense of providing an area of experience in which man's 'longing for a happier life; for humanity, goodness, joy, truth and solidarity'[1] can be realized without threatening the taboos and restrictions of capitalist society. Marcuse's own view, expressed in his *Eros and Civilization* (London 1969), is that Reich failed to make any essential distinction between repressive and non-repressive sublimation and that his sociological insights are vitiated by a 'sweeping primitivism': 'progress in freedom appears as a mere release in sexuality'. In fact, Reich's attitude to culture seems to have been simple-minded rather than primitive. In his view sexual satisfaction was a prerequisite of cultural and creative activity. 'The few bad poems which occasionally are created during abstinence are of no great interest' (*The Sexual Revolution*, p. 66).

4. Reich's idea that character-armour is represented by and is indeed in some sense identical with chronic muscular tensions will be discussed later in the chapter on vegetotherapy, since it was this observation, hypothesis or insight which led Reich to abandon psychoanalysis

1. Marcuse, H. 'The Affirmative Character of Culture' in *Negations*. London 1968.

and to experiment with physical forms of treatment.

5. The proposition that character-armour is the result of internalization of external pressures imposed by society and the family on individuals who under natural conditions would grow up healthy and sexually free, has already been discussed. But it is perhaps worth emphasizing that it constituted a major break with two of Freud's ideas; that of the death instinct which postulates the existence of an innate tendency in man towards morbidity, and that of the inherent weakness of the child's ego, which compels it to construct defences for its own sake, to protect itself from being overwhelmed by its own excessive instinctual impulses. As we shall see, Reich, during his later 'religious' phase, abandoned this environmental, sociological theory of the origin of character-armour, without however in any way reverting to Freud's position.

6. The first point to be made about Reich's idea that character-armour arises only within a specific authoritarian type of family is that it is a sociological or ideological concept, not a clinical finding. Reich is not maintaining that his psychoanalytical experience has led him to postulate a correlation between family structure and the neuroses of the constituent family members, or that all his cases displaying character-armour grew up in authoritarian families, in which the fathers oppressed their wives and children and repressed all manifestations of infantile sexuality. If he had, it would be possible to claim him as a pioneer of contemporary family psychiatry and to argue that he anticipated some of the findings that have been made by applying Gregory Bateson's 'double bind' theory of schizophrenia to families containing neurotic and psychotic members.

For it does indeed seem to be true that there are families which are held together not by parental love but by the exercise of power, and that such families produce neurotic and psychotic children in significant numbers. But it seems not to be true that in these families the pathogenic power is necessarily exercised by the father —indeed the literature contains many more references to dominating 'schizophrenogenic' and 'neurotogenic' mothers with weak husbands than to authoritarian fathers—or that repression of infantile sexuality is the only or even the main technique by which such parents exert power over their children, forcing them into neurotic submissiveness; indulgence, over-protectiveness and seductiveness seems to be just as efficient destructive weapons. Nor of course do appearances and realities necessarily coincide; a family can appear to be ruled by an authoritarian father when in fact it is dominated by a mother who prefers to rule from behind the throne.

However, Reich's idea that character-armour, and hence neurosis, was the result of internalization of the repressive, anti-libidinal values of the authoritarian family was not derived from clinical observation nor indeed adduced to explain clinical phenomena. It was introduced for two quite different reasons: to reconcile psychoanalysis and marxism, and to eliminate a discrepancy in marxist theory.

It was Reich's contention that the oppression of the masses by the ruling classes could not be explained by orthodox marxist theory, simply in terms of the material power wielded by the latter; the ruling classes were in his view only successful in controlling the masses because bourgeois society creates people with a character structure that renders them submissive towards authority and willing to be ruled by their rulers. 'Society is not the result of a certain psychic structure but the reverse is true; character structure is the result of a certain society' (*Character and Society*, p. 254). Furthermore, bourgeois society produces the character structure it requires through the mediation of various social institutions, notably the authoritarian family, the authoritarian school, and religion. 'From infancy on people are trained to be falsely modest, self-effacing and mechanically obedient, trained to suppress their natural instinctual energies' (*ibid*, p. 252). As a result, the character study of the majority 'corresponds to the interests of the political and economic rulers' (*The Sexual Revolution*, p. xx).

This formulation of the relationship between the structure of society, the structure of the family, and the character of the individual, had the merit of solving, to Reich's satisfaction at least, unresolved problems in both psychoanalysis and marxism. It provided an explanation of the origin of neurosis without recourse to fanciful biological theories such as the death instinct, and it resolved the discrepancy in marxist theory created by the fact, which was all too obvious during the rise of fascism, that the masses do not pursue the real economic interests of their own class, but are instead only too willing to follow authoritarian leaders.

It is not at all clear how Reich arrived at his idea that character structure, family structure and social structure are functionally correlated—'functionally identical' in his own terminology—but it can be seen as an example of his consistent application of what is nowadays usually called holistic thinking, which starts from the assumption that phenomena, including persons, are not discrete entities, complete and comprehensible in themselves—'no man is an island, entire of himself'—but are parts of larger wholes. Just as Arthur Koestler, who incidentally was in the same Communist Party cell as Reich in Berlin, postulates in his *The Ghost in the Machine* (London 1967) that all phenomena can be arranged in a hierarchy of holons (e.g. electrons, atoms, molecules, cells, organs, organisms, etc.), each of which can be regarded both as an entity in itself and as part of a larger, more complex controlling super-entity, so Reich thought of neurotic symptoms as part of a neurotic structure, which was itself part of a character structure, which was part of a family structure, which was part of a social structure, etc., the larger structure being socially or psychologically represented within its smaller, component units.

Although, as Paul A. Robinson points out in his *The Freudian Left*,[2] Reich's social theory 'offers an imaginative conceptual tool for sociological and historical research', which could be used 'to understand how economic realities are translated into politics, ethics and religion, indeed even to understand how the economic order itself is maintained', he in fact never worked it out in a way that was academically acceptable. 'The crude, undisciplined character of his mind did not lend itself to a patient empirical elaboration of his basic insight. In this respect, as in so many others, he fell short of the greatest social theorists, who never considered scholarly historical research beneath their dignity' (p. 45).

Incidentally, Reich's theory of orgasm is itself an example of holistic thinking, since it asserts simultaneously that orgasms are necessary for the physical and mental health of the individual considered as a single entity, and that to fulfil this function orgasms must be experienced in partnership with someone else. The need

2. New York 1969; published in London 1970, as *The Sexual Radicals*.

for orgastic experience is therefore the crucial biological evidence that human adults are not, autonomous, self-sufficient units who happen at times to relate to one another but are intrinsically members one of another. Reich was always insistent that masturbation is an inherently unsatisfying and tantalizing experience; 'in the long run it becomes unsatisfactory and quite disturbing because soon the lack of a love object becomes painful' (*The Sexual Revolution*, p. 110).

Although some of Reich's followers, notably the editors of *Reich Speaks of Freud*, have played down Reich's involvement with communism and marxism, even to the extent of claiming that it arose solely out of his interest in sexual hygiene, there can be no doubt that he was deeply committed to communism for several years. Although there are understandable reasons of political expediency for soft-pedalling the fact, he belonged to a generation of the intelligentsia, most of whose members were sympathetic towards communism. In the late 1920s and early 1930s it was not yet obvious that Leninism was turning into Stalinism or that the Soviet Union was going to emerge as yet another imperialist power.

7. One of the difficulties of the marxist position in general and of Reich's version of it in particular is that of knowing how much reality can be attached to its widest abstractions. It is not hard to attach meaning to concepts such as 'character structure', 'the family', authoritarian or otherwise, 'the state', 'class', but it is much less easy to be sure that there is such an entity as 'bourgeois society', or to know what social or historical phenomena are legitimately embraced by such a concept as the 'patriarchal authoritarian culture' which according to Reich has been in existence for the last 4–6,000 years. This is indeed one of Reich's most peculiar ideas

and it will require a brief excursion into the history of anthropology if we are to understand how he came to entertain it.

According to Reich's theory of the origin of contemporary society and its neuroses, the original 'natural' society was matriarchal. Politically, this society lacked any system of domination; sexually, it was entirely permissive. Since fathers had no power, children had no Oedipus complex, repression did not occur and everyone was happy, free and spontaneous. Although this idea is patently a fantasy, Reich seems really to have believed that such an idyllic state of affairs did once exist. 'In primitive society, which has a collective and work-democratic organization, the unit is the clan, comprising all the blood relatives of a common mother. Within this clan, which is also the economic unit, there is no other marriage than the loose ties of a sexual relationship.' However, as a result of unexplained economic changes, matriarchy is gradually replaced by patriarchy and 'natural sexual sociality is replaced by the demands of morality; voluntary, happy, love relationship is replaced by "marital duty" ... sex-economically regulated life is replaced by genital repression, neurotic disturbances and sexual perversions; the naturally strong, self-reliant biological organism becomes weak, helpless, dependent, fearful of God; the orgastic experiencing of nature is replaced by mystical ecstasy ...' (*The Sexual Revolution*, pp. 161–2).

One only has to ask where this matriarchal society was, when it existed, and what records of it survive, to realize that this is anthropological fantasy, bearing no relation to historical reality. But to be fair to Reich, it is no more a fantasy than is Freud's account in *Totem and Taboo* of the origin of the Oedipus complex and of neurotic guilt in the murder of the Primal Father by his rebellious sons. And to be fair to both of them, it must be added that they were both engaging in a form of speculative activity, which was accepted as legitimate at the time, but which has been invalidated by subsequent developments in anthropology.

They were in fact constructing fantasies based on two assumptions, which were accepted by the majority of nineteenth-century anthropologists, but which are rejected by all contemporary anthropologists, whether functional or structural.

The first assumption is that the concept of evolution can be applied directly to human societies. This idea, which derives from Spencer, leads to the further sub-assumptions that some societies are 'primitive' and others evolved or 'advanced', and that existing 'primitive' societies provide evidence of what advanced societies were like before they evolved. The analogy is, of course, with biology. The fact that fishes, amphibia, reptiles and mammals can be arranged in an evolutionary series, 'the diapason closing full in man' (Dryden), and that there are still fishes, reptiles, etc., alive in a world apparently dominated by man, was used to justify the idea that 'primitive', i.e. non-European societies, were survivals from earlier phases in the evolution of 'civilized', i.e. European, man. Furthermore, since many of these so-called primitive societies hold beliefs which strike Western intellectuals as irrational and illogical, attempts were made to explain these as early evolutionary stages in the development of the capacity for logical and rational thinking. And on the basis of the biological law that ontogeny recapitulates phylogeny, parallels were drawn between the minds of savages and those of European, usually middle class, children. As Roger S. Poole puts it in his Introduction to the English translation of Lévi-Strauss's *Totemism* (London 1969) 'It was a question of fitting together savage fancy with civilized fact, and no one at the time seemed even the slightest bit embarrassed by this appalling presumption. Progressivist and evolutionist superiority then, the belief in the linear advance of civilization, the belief in the search for origins, the assumption that all logics should operate according to the same axes of signification, such was the picture of nineteenth-century and some twentieth-century speculation.'

The second assumption made by both Freud, when he traced the origins of the Oedipus complex back to a primal, patriarchal horde, and by Reich, when he asserted that the earliest human society was matriarchal, was that the conventions governing kinship and the tracing of lineages reflect the structure of a society and the nature of the power relationships existing within it. According to this assumption, the fact that, as was originally believed, all 'primitive' societies are patrilineal, i.e. trace lineages and define kinship relationships through the male line, was regarded as valid evidence that all societies are ruled by men and that this had always been so.

However, this rather simple view of the matter did not survive detailed and systematic investigation of specific societies made by anthropologists who actually went to live in them, instead of just staying, as for instance Frazer did, in their studies collating evidence derived from travellers' tales. It then turned out not only that kinship rules and social structures were much more varied and complicated than had previously been realized, and that societies, which resembled one another in being in the widest sense patrilineal, might have very different social organizations, but also that some societies were matrilineal, tracing lineage and kinship primarily through the female line.

It was this latter fact that Reich seized upon to construct his theory that natural, primitive society is matriarchal. Following Bachofen, Morgan and Engels he assumed that matrilineal societies were matriarchal, and argued that they represented survivals from an earlier stage of human evolutionary development corresponding to Marx's era of primitive communism, in which there had been no state, no private property and no sexual repression.

In support of this thesis Reich made considerable use of Malinowski's studies of the Trobriand Islanders of Melanesia.[3] Among the Trobriand Islanders descent is matrilineal, physiological paternity is not acknowledged, and there are no social restraints imposed upon the sexual activities of either children or of adolescents and adults prior to marriage. They seemed indeed to have no Oedipus complex, no sexual repressions, and to provide convincing evidence with which to refute Freud's pessimistic view that guilt and repression were the result of an innate, phylogenetically determined Oedipus complex and were therefore inescapable aspects of the human condition. As a result Reich cited Malinowski's work in support of his contention that ' "savages" show a sex-economy which is far superior to ours' (*The Sexual Revolution*, p. 131) and used the idea that there exist sexually permissive, primitive matriarchal societies to support his thesis that his sexual paradise was practical politics. It already existed in Melanesia, it had occurred in pre-history; it could therefore be intro-

3. Malinowski, B., *The Sexual Life of Savages in North Western Melanesia*. London 1929.

duced into 'advanced' societies after the Sexual Revolution.

Reich was, however, wrong on one essential point. Although the Trobriand Islanders are matrilineal, their society is not matriarchal and Malinowski himself never suggested that it was. Nor did he use his researches to support evolutionary speculations about the original nature of human society. Indeed as a functional anthropologist he did not consider such speculations legitimate. In his view the customs and beliefs of the Trobriand Islanders needed to be explained in terms of their function within the totality of their culture, not in terms of any social-evolutionary theory. So in using Malinowski's evidence to construct a theory about the nature of natural, primitive society, Reich was misunderstanding Malinowski's work and being old-fashioned into the bargain. Reich's misuse of Malinowski's researches is indeed an excellent example of the way in which Reich looked for data to support theses, instead of constructing theories to explain facts.

In fact power in matrilineal societies still resides with the men, and men still exert authority over children. Malinowski himself described the frictions that arise between Trobriand fathers and their brothers-in-law over the discipline and future careers of their sons-nephews, and there seems to be no doubt that the whole idea of matriarchy is a myth. As Robin Fox puts in his *Kinship and Marriage* (London 1967), 'The whole problem with matrilineal systems [is] ... how to combine continuity and recruitment through females with control by the *men* of the lineage.' Fox goes on to point out that for most men the idea of matriarchy conjures up an Amazonian world in which 'men would be of no account and would be used for breeding purposes only.

55

Such a sinister practice exists only in the imagination, although most people have at some time or other accused their neighbours of it, or at least of being in some way 'matriarchal'. Thus Athens accused Sparta, France accused England, and now we are accusing the Americans. It probably arises from a deep-rooted fear on the part of men that they will lose their position, and the fear is projected onto disliked nations. Be this as it may, the true Amazonian solution is unknown. Women don't ever seem to have got quite such a grip on things.'

Reich was therefore most unusual in idealizing matriarchy and in conceiving of women solely as sources of love and not at all as threatening dominators. His whole political, social and sexual stance can indeed be interpreted as a massive rejection or dismissal of the problem of dominance in human relationships. It was, he believed, possible to conceive of a world in which nobody dominated anyone in any way whatsoever. One again wonders what he would have made of the recent ethological work which suggests that the establishment of hierarchies, in which each member of a group has and knows his place, is one of the basic biological mechanisms for maintaining peace and cohesion within groups. It appears however that the impulse to dominate was clearly visible in Reich's own character.

4 The Sexual Revolution

In the previous chapter I remarked that Reich was a practical man and it is a striking fact that many of the specific reforms he recommended in *The Function of the Orgasm* and *The Sexual Revolution* are perfectly sensible and reasonable, and can often be justified on simple grounds of humanity without needing the support of theoretical and ideological constructions. In particular, he displays great understanding of the crippling effects of poverty and lack of privacy on human relationships.

However Reich was a typical central European intellectual in believing that no idea was satisfactorily stated until it had been underpinned by an impressive theoretical substructure and been clearly placed in its appropriate position in a completely formulated *Weltanschauung*. Furthermore, as a doctor and an adherent of Freud's idea that psychology should be based on the natural sciences, he believed that all propositions about human nature should be formulated in terms that at least sound scientific. As a result all the reforms proposed by Reich to bring about his Sexual Revolution are presented, scientifically, as logical deductions from his theory of sex economy and, medically, as prophylactic measures for the prevention of neurosis.

Since, according to Reich, 'the plague of the neuroses is bred during three principal phases of life', childhood, puberty and adulthood, his proposals are best considered under these three headings.

1. *Childhood.* In Reich's view the two factors in childhood most productive of neurosis were strict and premature house-training and the prohibition of childhood masturbation. Although Reich, with his sexological bias, can hardly be said to have emphasized the point, he nonetheless consistently held that strict house-training is harmful. In doing so he was affirming an idea generally accepted in the psychoanalytical circles of his time. As I mentioned earlier, the idea that 'character' could be a defence first arose in psychoanalysis in connection with anal erotism, the development of the obsessional character, with its triad of compulsive obstinacy, orderliness and parsimony, being attributed to severe and early house-training. A case could be made out for maintaining that the whole of Reich's work on character-armour is really a study of the pervasive individual and social effects of obsessional defences. Many analysts who are totally uninfluenced by Reich are ready to agree that bourgeois society is basically obsessional, though not all of them would go on to argue that this is necessarily a bad thing. The issue raised by Reich as to whether human beings can do without character-armour or obsessional defences, and can rely instead on an inherent tendency to self-regulation, is by no means dead in psychoanalytical circles, and has recently been raised again, though in less specifically sexual or anal terms, by both Laing and Winnicott in their writings on the true and false self.

Here it must be mentioned that, psychoanalytically speaking, Reich was very much a child of his own times in not discussing the role of the early oral attachment to the mother in the causation of neurosis. Psychoanalysis only became interested in the first year of life after Reich had ceased to be connected with it, and the pioneers in this field, Melanie Klein and Winnicott, worked in London, not in Vienna. Since contemporary research into the infant's early relationship with its mother has led to increasing awareness of the importance of grief, depression and despair in both normal and neurotic development, Reich's remarkable obliviousness to this aspect of human experience, which shows up perhaps most noticeably in his habit of discussing sexual relationships without mentioning the grief and sense of loss which attends their termination, can be interpreted historically as a reflection of the state of psychoanalysis in Vienna in the 1920s. It is however impossible not to wonder whether it was also part of his own personal need to deny the implications of the premature deaths of his own parents.

However, despite Reich's failure to consider the possible role of disturbances in the original mother–infant relationship in breeding neurosis, it can be surmised with some confidence that his anti-authoritarian attitude would have led him to disapprove of feeding by the clock, that his belief in spontaneity in all things would have made him an advocate of demand feeding, and that his faith in instinct would have made him a believer in close and continuous physical intimacy between mothers and their infants.

Reich's objection to the prohibition of infantile masturbation arose primarily from his conviction that 'the inhibition of infantile sexuality is the basis for the fixation to parental home and its atmosphere, the "family". It is the origin of the typical lack of independence in thought and action' (*The Function of the Orgasm*, pp. 171–2). It was in his view the prime example of 'the killing of spontaneous vital impulses by the process of education in the interest of dubious refinement' (*ibid.*, p. 192).

However, despite his conviction that suppression of infantile sexuality was the main source of western man's submissiveness and lack of spontaneity, he did not hold that all infantile masturbation is in fact healthy and spontaneous. On the contrary, he seems to have been one of the first psychoanalysts to appreciate how often it is a compulsive symptom and is engendered by conflict and not by desire. In *The Sexual Revolution* (p. 245) he quoted with approval the observation of the Russian psychoanalyst Vera Schmitt, who ran a children's home in Moscow in the early 1920s, that there are two forms of childhood masturbation; one which is spontaneous and genuinely erotic, and another which is 'a reaction to an insult, a disparagement or a limitation of freedom'. Reich's recognition of the importance of this distinction goes hand in hand with his insistence that much of what passes for normal sexual activity among European adults is really a compulsive, neurotic symptom, impelled by anxiety and sadism, not by genuine sexual desire.

2. *Puberty*. Reich's views on puberty as a phase of life during which neuroses are created were based on the simple and straightforward premise that '*puberty signifies coming into sexual maturity*, and primarily nothing else' (*The Function of the Orgasm*, p. 173. Reich's italics). Since according to sex-economic principles sexual abstinence produces sexual stasis, and sexual stasis reactivates infantile neurotic patterns of behaviour, Reich advocated complete sexual freedom for all young persons above the age of fifteen. 'What is at stake is the gratification of the physical needs of ripening

youth ... sexual happiness of maturing youth is a central issue in the prevention of the neuroses' (*ibid.*, p. 173). In his view the prohibitions and restraints imposed on the sexual activities of adolescents not only caused an enormous amount of frustration and misery at the time, but also had permanent and crippling effects on the personality; these crippling effects being indeed the reason why the prohibitions were imposed. Their social function was to make each new generation submissive and conformist and, in particular, sufficiently inhibited to accept meekly the limitations on orgastic satisfaction imposed by the institution of monogamous 'compulsive marriage'; while the motive underlying the imposition was 'the older generation's fear of youth's sexuality and fighting spirit' (*ibid.*, p. 173).

Reich's analysis of the problem of puberty in Chapter VI of *The Sexual Revolution* is a vivid and in many ways understanding account of the predicament of sexually awakened young people growing up in a culture which demands sexual abstinence for several years after puberty. Too much of it is as applicable today as it was in 1930, when the original German version was published. Indeed, if it were true that 'puberty signifies coming into sexual maturity, *and primarily nothing else,*' (my italics this time) Reich's position would be unassailable. But in fact and as usual Reich's whole method of argument begs all the difficult questions—this time in two different ways.

First, even if it were true that in his much-beloved primitive, matriarchal societies 'sexual misery is unknown' (*The Sexual Revolution*, p. 81), the onus is really on Reich to show that this freedom from sexual misery is not purchased at a price, i.e. to demonstrate that there is no functional connection or correlation between the development of the hygienic, cultural and aesthetic amenities of literate and technologically advanced civilizations and the postponement for educational purposes of adult status for some years after puberty. Any thorough comparison of the degrees of sexual happiness or misery experienced by members of different cultures would have to take into account the relationship of their sexual customs to all other non-sexual aspects of the cultures, including both the availability or otherwise of other forms of satisfaction and the average duration of life. Perhaps Melanesians do enjoy an adolescence without sexual frustration and misery, but I doubt whether they live as long as we do.

There is also the question of the quality of love, and in particular of the romantic ideal of 'falling in love', which our society values highly (though perhaps decreasingly so), but which is rare elsewhere and is generally regarded outside Western Europe and the United States as a socially disruptive phenomenon.[1] When one considers the amount of intense happiness and misery experienced by young people who fall in love, one realizes that it would require a more subtle exponent of hedonic calculus than Reich to decide whether his sort of sexual freedom would increase or decrease the total sum of human happiness. Reich, however, blocks all discussion of these real and still open issues by his blanket assumption that all sexual repression is a technique of social oppression.

The second way in which Reich begs the question is by making the *a priori* assumption that all adolescents, who do not actively seek sexual intercourse the moment they reach puberty, are neurotic. This assumption en-

1. See Geoffrey Gorer's essay 'On Falling in Love' in *The Danger of Equality*, London 1966.

ables him to use apparent evidence against his thesis as evidence for it, without having to prove that he is entitled to do so. In Reich's view all teenagers who do not have sexual intercourse from the age of fifteen onwards, refrain from doing so out of fear of their parents and are persons 'without ambition, submissive' (*The Sexual Revolution*, p. 83). I doubt whether this is true; some are just not ready for it. It seems to be a characteristic of our culture that psychological and emotional development often lags behind physical maturation, so that sexual awakening often occurs an appreciable time after puberty. To assume, as Reich does, that this lag is necessarily a symptom of neurosis seems to me to be a typical Reichian over-simplification and abuse of psychopathology. It involves the same fallacy as the 'crude' marxist idea that artistic and cultural movements are mere epiphenomenal reflections of economic and class interests without any historical dynamic of their own. It also assumes that orgastic satisfaction is an aim that can be pursued in isolation from all the other needs which draw human beings towards one another.

Reich also makes things easy for himself in a number of other ways. He completely ignores friendships between members of the same sex, and indeed everything that can be related to the homosexual component of human nature. This is a remarkable omission when one considers the extent to which the education of adolescents has been, and still largely remains, a process by which knowledge, skills and cultural attitudes are transmitted from one generation to another by relationships between teachers and pupils of the same sex. He also assumes that contraceptives are always reliable, which they certainly weren't in the 1930s, and as a result he largely ignores all problems related to pregnancy, childbirth and abortion. Indeed, despite all his sympathy for the young and sexually frustrated, and despite too his pose of being down to earth, *The Sexual Revolution* conjures up a bleak and curiously unreal picture of adolescence. In Reich's vision all young people are lonely and longing, none of them have brothers and sisters or friends, and none of them are fond of their parents. The generation gap is always absolute, no parent ever remembering what it was like to be young, and no young person ever enjoying the company of his parents.

3. *Adulthood.* In Reich's view the most fertile soil of neurosis in adulthood was 'compulsive marriage', by which he meant conventional, monogamous, 'bourgeois' marriage. In his opinion this form of human relationship was emphatically not an expression of any natural need for continuity and permanence in human companionship or for mutual enjoyment of parenthood, but was 'the form into which sexual needs were forced by socioeconomic processes. Sexual and economic needs, especially on the part of the women, merge into the desire for marriage, apart from the ideology acquired in early childhood and the moral pressure of society' (*The Function of the Orgasm*, p. 174). Despite the fact that according to Reich's theories the social function of both repression of infantile sexuality and of the restrictions imposed on the sexual life of adolescents was to construct a type of personality which would find compulsive marriage acceptable if not actively enjoyable, his critique of bourgeois marriage is basically that these preparations for it are ineffective. As a result 'every marriage sickens as a result of an ever-increasing conflict between sexual and economic needs. The sexual needs can be satisfied with

one and the same partner only for a limited period of time. Economic dependence, moral demands, and habituations, on the other hand, work towards permanence of the relationship. This conflict is the basis of marital misery' (*ibid.*, pp. 174–5).

It must be noted that Reich has here insinuated into his argument a commonly held, but scientifically unproven, assumption about human nature, viz. that both men and women are naturally polygamous. As a result they inevitably tire of 'one and the same partner' after a 'limited period of time'. He then takes this assumption as proved and proceeds 'Full sexual capacity can make marriage happy. But the same capacity is at variance with every aspect of the moralistic demands for a lifelong monogamous marriage. This is a fact and nothing but a fact.'

The same point is made at greater length in *The Sexual Revolution*: 'Marriages could be good, at least for a certain period of time, if there were sexual harmony and gratification. This would, however, presuppose a sex-affirmative education, premarital sexual experience, and emancipation from conventional morality. But the very thing that might make for a good marriage means at the same time its doom. For once sexuality is affirmed, once moralism is overcome, there is no longer any inner argument against intercourse with other partners except for a period of time, during which faithfulness based on gratification exists (but not for a life-time). The ideology of marriage collapses and with it the marriage. It is no longer marriage, but a permanent sexual relationship. Such a relationship, because of the absence of suppression of genital desires, is more apt to prove happy than strictly monogamous marriage. In many cases, the cure for an unhappy marriage—moralists and authoritarian law notwithstanding—is marital infidelity' (p. 144).

This idea that full sexual capacity and monogamy are incompatible led Reich to speak of an 'inherent contradiction in the institution of marriage'. In view of Reich's remarkable sense of certitude about what are, after all merely his own personal opinions—the mind boggles at the idea of constructing a scientific demonstration that man is naturally polygamous (heterotropic) and that monogamous (monotropic) behaviour is pathological, or alternatively that man is naturally monogamous and all polygamous behaviour is pathological—it is not surprising that he was even prepared to make a definite statement about the average duration of natural 'permanent sexual relationships' : they last for four years (*The Sexual Revolution*, pp. 139–40).

Similarly, and equally rashly, Reich also commits himself to a definite statement about the orgastic needs of healthy genital characters. 'Biologically speaking the healthy human organism calls for three to four thousand sexual acts in the course of a sexual life of, say, thirty to forty years.' (*The Function of the Orgasm*, p. 175). To save readers the trouble of working out the mathematics of this statement, it means that genital characters average between 75 and 133 orgasms a year, figures which are modest by contemporary Kinsey ratings. They also imply, bearing in mind Reich's view that sexual life begins at fifteen, that orgastic capacity disappears between the ages of 45 and 55, a curiously Victorian idea to come from a sexual enthusiast. But Reich never seems to have concerned himself with the psychology or sexual physiology of the middle-aged and old.

The sexual revolution envisaged and proclaimed by

Reich would consist therefore in the social recognition of the importance and value of 'permanent sexual relationships', existing solely for the mutual orgastic gratification of the two partners to it, and clearly differentiated from marriage as a social and economic contract. It would indeed amount to a total severance of the historical links between marriage as a legal institution concerned with the support and protection of women and children, and with the inheritance of property, and marriage as a public affirmation of mutual love. As Reich himself saw clearly, such a revolution would presuppose radical changes of both a social and psychological kind.

Socially it presupposes a world in which women are economically independent, either by being able to earn their own livings or by receiving state subsidies for the maintenance of their children, in which fathers play a relatively unimportant role in the lives of their children, and in which crèches and nursery schools are available for the children of working mothers. Psychologically, it demands the elimination of possessiveness in human relationships. In Reich's view jealousy was a natural emotion—'It is absolutely natural to suffer pain at the thought of the beloved partner in somebody else's arms' —but he also believed that it is equally unnatural to seek to prevent a former partner from starting a relationship with someone else. This is another example of Reich's belief that the exercise of power is not an essential aspect of human nature.

Since there are today circles in most metropolitan areas of Western Europe and the U.S.A. in which something approximating to the sexual revolution has already occurred, and has done so without any accompanying economic revolution, it must be emphasized that Reich formulated his theory of sex economy in the

1930s and that at least three social changes have taken place in the intervening years, which neither he nor any of his marxist contemporaries anticipated. First, capitalism, so far from being in its death throes, has shown itself capable of surviving a world war without radical changes in the distribution of power between classes. Secondly, in highly industrialized countries capitalism has entered into a phase not predicted by Marx, in which class power is maintained not by force and poverty but by the persuasive powers of the mass media and by the provision of material affluence for the more articulate sections of the population, e.g. salaried workers, the professions and business executives, who remain nonetheless excluded from real power. As a result the revolutionary impetus resides not, as pre-war marxists believed, in the proletariat and other 'progressive elements' of technologically advanced industrial societies, but in rural, developing areas such as Africa, Asia and Latin America. And thirdly, the correlation between class structure and sexual morality has proved, in industrial societies at least, to be less close than Reich believed; permissive sexual morality seems to offer little threat to bourgeois property relationships. The invention and commercial exploitation of reliable contraceptives is a major cause of this last unexpected development.

Finally, it must be added that neuroses and sexual inhibitions (hang-ups) are far from being unknown in circles which distinguish clearly between marriage as a legal institution and 'permanent sexual relationships.' In such circles the neuroses of frustration have, it seems, been replaced by neuroses of confusion. And the economic independence of the women involved is often not based on their freedom to work and earn money but on alimony or unearned, inherited incomes. Indeed, as many observers have pointed out, the sexual revolution has so far at least proved to be largely an upper middle-class phenomenon having little if anything to do with the class war.

5 Vegetotherapy

In the previous chapter I mentioned that one of the
fundamental principles of Reich's theory of sex-economy is the idea that character-armour is represented
somatically in muscular tensions and various stereotyped postures and gestures; in other words, that character-armour is accompanied by, or in Reich's own rather
curious terminology is 'functionally identical' with
'muscular-armour'. This idea, hypothesis or insight—it is
difficult to decide which word to use—that the overcon-
trolled, inhibited, unspontaneous character-neurotic is
also literally a rigid, tense, unrelaxed person led Reich to
make a step in therapy which constituted a final break
with psychoanalysis, since it occurred to him that it
might be possible to attack the character-defence
directly through the body. If by appropriate manipula-
tion of his muscular-armour the patient was rendered
incapable of sustaining his defences against the spontaneous expression of emotion, these would be released
—and the long, arduous and not always successful psychological techniques of defence—and character-analysis
could be either replaced or supplemented by a direct
physical approach to the patient's person.

Although, when expressed in such simple terms, this
new therapeutic technique, which Reich called vegetotherapy, sounds in no way startling or outrageous, it
constituted a complete break with the psychoanalytical
tradition that psychoanalysis is a 'talking cure', in which
the analyst maintains his physical and psychological dis-

tance from the patient, this distancing being justified on two theoretical grounds; that neuroses are psychological illnesses and are therefore only appropriately treated by psychological techniques, and that the analyst must preserve his anonymity, or rather unactuality, as a person in order to ensure that all the patient's reactions to him can be interpreted as transference phenomena, i.e. as revivals of past feelings of love and hate towards the significant figures in his childhood and not as direct, actual responses to his present therapist's behaviour.

There seems to be well authenticated evidence that this new technique of Reich's was at times highly successful. Both the English educationalist A. S. Neill and the Norwegian psychiatrist Nic Waal vouch for its effectiveness on themselves and on others. (See *Wilhelm Reich*, ed. P. Ritter) A. S. Neill writes: 'All I need say here about it is that I got more emotional reaction and relief after six weeks of his therapy than I'd had in several years of talkie analysis. It was no picnic; it meant many a painful hour. I was possibly too old to get the full benefit of the treatment, but on the other hand I gained something more important to me—the friendship of a warm, sincere, brilliant man' (Ritter, p. 21); while Nic Waal, who like Neill had also had previous experience of 'talkie analysis', writes 'he detected at once—quite unlike my previous therapists—that I had used a lively and vital erotism as a defence against aggression and depression. He detected at once also that I had severe problems around aggression, that I was falsely kind and a false "yes-sayer". It was a terrible revelation, but I knew he was right, that what I had fought for theoretically and personally was really a true fight. I could stand being crushed by Reich because I liked truth. And strangely enough, I was

71

not crushed by it. All through this therapeutic attitude to me, he had a loving voice, he sat beside me and made me look at him. He accepted me and crushed only my vanity and falseness. But I understood at that moment that true honesty and love both in a therapist and in parents is sometimes the courage to be seemingly cruel when it is necessary. It demands, however, a great deal of the therapist, his training and his diagnosis of the patient' (Ritter, p. 43). However, despite her own enthusiastic and grateful personal response to Reich, Nic Waal goes on to voice her professional misgivings about his very direct approach towards his patients. 'I am not sure that Reich really always had the tool at that time to diagnose the patient, when unfolding his cruel and penetrating technique. I do not think he was detached from what happened to him to go through this necessary therapeutic diagnosis towards all those, to whom he gave therapy. Some became either crushed or obsessively oppositional or projective by his active therapy. But many were rescued from severe personality problems' (Ritter, p. 43–4).

Both these quotations show that vegetotherapy with Reich was a highly dramatic, direct encounter with Reich's personality, and that its effectiveness depended as much on the patient's capacity to believe that Reich radiated love as on any theories which Reich as a scientist might happen to be holding at the time. And it is at this point in the development of Reich's ideas that his theories begin to become peculiar, to put it mildly. Incidentally, neither Neill nor Nic Waal followed Reich in his later move from vegetotherapy to orgone therapy, although both remained personally loyal and attached to him.

Reich's own account of vegetotherapy is given in

Chapter VIII of the 1942 edition of *The Function of the Orgasm*. Contemporary readers, particularly if they are not medically trained, will have difficulties with it, since much of its theoretical formulation is based on a number of assumptions about the nature and function of what in the 1930s and 1940s was commonly known as the Vegetative Nervous System—i.e. that part of the nervous system which is NOT subject to voluntary control and which innervates those organs such as the heart, intestines and genitals which are not capable of being affected directly by acts of will. This system, which is now usually called the autonomic nervous system, is divided into two parts, the sympathetic and parasympathetic systems, and Reich persuaded himself that it was possible to establish a direct correlation between parasympathetic activity and pleasure on the one hand and between sympathetic activity and anxiety on the other. It seems indeed that he believed that the Unconscious was located in the parasympathetic system, and that this belief satisfied his early expressed wish to find something tangible corresponding to every idea. Vegetotherapy was therefore rationalized theoretically as an attempt to liberate the expansive, pleasure-giving, outgoing, life-enhancing forces contained in the parasympathetic vegetative centres from the restrictive, shrinking, inhibiting effects of sympathetic stimulation. In typical Reichian manner, this presumed antagonism between the two systems was epitomized in slogans : the parasympathetic nervous system stood for 'Toward the world, out of the self' and the sympathetic nervous system stood for 'Away from the world, back into the self'.

However, this vegetative theory need not be taken too seriously, since Reich himself offends against it in two different ways. He frequently uses the word 'vegetative' in an entirely arbitrary, private sense of his own to describe 'good' ideas such as 'natural', 'spontaneous' 'sexual', quite regardless of the possible neurophysiological processes which may or may not be involved in what he is describing. And much of his actual 'vegetotherapy' was concerned with 'muscular-armour' phenomena occurring in voluntary muscles which are not innervated by the vegetative (autonomic) nervous system at all.

A further difficulty which will disturb all but the most devoted Reichians is that his account of vegetotherapy contains a number of dogmatic, categorical statements of such improbability that one is tempted to dismiss the whole chapter as nonsensical. For instance, on page 275 of the 1942 edition he asserts that inhibition of respiration is 'the basic mechanism of the neurosis in general', since 'if respiration is reduced, less oxygen is introduced ... a smaller amount of energy is created in the organism, the vegetative impulses are less intense and consequently easier to master.' In other words, neurotics use as their primary defence mechanism the technique of reducing their vitality by breathing in less oxygen. An even more preposterous notion is his idea, based on very shaky biological speculations about the orgastic longings of protozoa, that human orgasm includes an attempt to become spherical, an attempt which man's possession of a backbone dooms to failure. How Reich arrived at such an idea, or why he should have wanted to maintain it, are entirely baffling problems, though as students of mysticism and theology know, Reich was not the first person to voice the existence of a wish to be spherical. According to an early Christian heresy at the resurrection we will arise from the dead in the form of perfect spheres.

However, if one is capable of surmounting these vari-

ous obstacles to taking Reich seriously, his account of
vegetotherapy is not without interest and the technique
is not as foolish as its theoretical trimmings. Starting
from the two basic assumptions that (1) the aim of
therapy is the release and restoration of the orgasm
reflex, and (2) 'every muscular rigidity contains the history and the meaning of its origin' (p. 267), Reich
proceeded by picking on some stereotyped facial expression of the patient's and interfering with it, by, for instance, continually drawing the patient's attention to it,
making him exaggerate it or adopt by an act of will the
reverse expression. This apparently had two effects. The
stereotyped expression gradually became comprehensible as a compromise between two opposed forces; the
wish to express an emotion, usually of anger or sorrow,
and the wish to prevent its expression. Interpretation of
this conflict eventually led to expression of the previously repressed emotion and later to the patient remembering the childhood traumatic experience which had
engendered the emotion and at the same time had neces-
sitated its repression. Secondly, tensions and rigidities in
the patient's chest and abdomen gradually became visible
and palpable. (It is not explicitly stated to what extent
his patients were undressed at this stage in the proceedings, but Reich writes throughout as though their whole
bodies were visible to him and he several times reports
himself as palpating muscles and viscera.) These chest,
abdominal and, later, pelvic tensions were then dealt
with as the earlier facial ones had been—and with similar releases of anger or tears. Then at some point in the
proceedings the patient began to report pleasurable and
often unequivocally sexual sensations. These were the
first signs of the emergent orgasm reflex breaking out of
the character-armour. In the one case which Reich de-

scribes in detail 'From then on, the work was concentrated upon having the patient give a detailed description of his behaviour in the sexual act' and therapy came to a successful conclusion when the patient 'reported with great surprise that during intercourse his pelvis had moved "so peculiarly *by itself*".' (p. 290.)

Characteristically, Reich remains silent both about the patient's physical and psychological responses to being looked at and touched by his therapist, and about the therapist's responses to the increasing relaxation, trustfulness and overt sexual behaviour of his patients. He writes, as twenty-five years later Masters and Johnson have done, as though it were possible for a therapist to remain objective, unmoved and yet human when confronted with the overt sexual reactions of his patients. As a result it is impossible to decide to what extent the effectiveness of such direct onslaughts on sexual inhibition depends on the therapist's correct understanding of the psychological and physiological principles involved or on some charismatic factor in his personality which enables him to bless the patient sexually by a secular, pseudo-medical form of the religious ceremony of Laying On Of Hands (Confirmation).

Incidentally, Reich, unlike Masters and Johnson, does not appear to have found it necessary to supply 'surrogate partners' for patients without partners. (In their recent *Human Sexual Inadequacy* (Boston, 1970) Masters and Johnson report doing so occasionally for unattached males who apply for treatment at the Reproductive Biology Research Foundation, St Louis.)

In view of Reich's later development, his account of vegetotherapy contains one detail of great significance.

This is that, concurrently with the dissolution of their character and muscular-armours and the emergence of their true orgastic capacity, his patients regularly recovered a 'feeling of depth and earnestness, which was lost long ago ... patients recall that period in their early childhood in which the unity of their bodily sensations was as yet undisturbed. Deeply moved, they relate how, as small children, they felt one with nature, with everything around them, how they felt 'alive', and how all this was subsequently broken to pieces and destroyed by their training. This breaking up of the unity of bodily feelings through sexual suppression, and the constant longing to re-establish contact with the self and with the world, is the subjective basis of all sex-negating religions. 'God' is the mystical idea of the vegetative harmony of the self with nature. If and when God represents nothing but the personification of the natural laws which govern man and make him part of the universal natural process, then—and only then—can natural science and religion come to terms' (*The Function of the Orgasm*, p. 319).

In this passage Reich is, I think, doing something more than describe the loss of the neurotic sense of alienation which occurs at the end of all successful psychotherapies, though I suspect that some of his patients would have been prepared to leave it at that; he is also proclaiming his own conviction that he had at last discovered, by what in his own view was a pure natural-scientific route the rational basis of his earlier intimations of the oneness of self and nature and the reconcilability of Freud's mechanistic view of man and Bergson's vitalism.

It would, I think, have been better for Reich's reputation if he had stopped here and had contented himself with asserting that successful psychotherapy leads patients to a view of their relationship to nature which resembles the religious conception of pantheism. However, intransigent as ever, Reich felt obliged to search for some physical process by which this sense of the harmony between self and nature was mediated. As a young man, in the early 1920s, Reich had maintained that 'there was no denying the principle of a creative power governing life; only it was not satisfactory as long as it was not tangible, as long as it could not be described or practically handled.' In the late 1930s and early 1940s, following a number of very peculiar and unconvincing experiments conducted during the course of practising vegetotherapy, Reich succeeded in persuading himself that he had indeed discovered something tangible which is present in both man and nature, which pervades the cosmos, and which is the active force responsible for man's longing for orgastic and mystical union with the Other. This something tangible, Reich called 'orgone energy', 'bio-energy' or 'primordial cosmic energy'; it was, he claimed not only universally present but also universally demonstrable; it could be seen under a microscope and its activities recorded with thermometers, electroscopes and Geiger–Mueller counters. It is, however, impossible to take this 'discovery' of Reich's seriously, since he also maintained that 'orgone energy' is a different sort of substance or phenomenon to those which microscopes, thermometers, electroscopes and Geiger–Mueller counters are constructed to observe and measure. In other words, he maintained that he had discovered a form of energy different in quality from the kind of energy with which the natural sciences concern themselves, but justified his 'discovery' by an appeal to natural-scientific techniques. It is not surprising therefore that no scientist of any standing or merit has ever taken the slightest notice of Reich's researches, or that several of his friends, notably A. S. Neill and Nic Waals, went out of their way to assert their incompetence to pass judgment on his later work—or that his enemies dismissed his orgone theory as a paranoid delusional system and used it as evidence that he had been crazy all along.

There is, however, a more interesting and also more charitable way of approaching the system of ideas developed by Reich in his later years. This is to regard it not, as Reich himself claimed, as a scientific theory based on experimental researches, but as a philosophy of life, a *Weltanschauung*, perhaps even a cosmology or theology, which Reich arrived at by some unrecorded inner, private process of development. As I mentioned in my first chapter, in one respect Reich did not live up to his claim to have stepped 'beyond the intellectual framework of present-day human character structure'; he never questioned the idea that rationalism and the natural sciences are the only avenue to the truth. As a result he formulated his system of ideas as though he had arrived at them by scientific techniques of observation and inference, a piece of self-deception which led him to exaggerate the originality of his ideas and to ignore their similarity to ideas which recurrently through history have been expressed by poets and mystics—and into making a number of very bizarre statements which, particularly when quoted out of context, do indeed often sound crazy.

In view of my conviction that the system of ideas which Reich himself styled the science of orgonomy really belongs to theology and mysticism and not to science, I shall attempt in the next chapter to describe them in a way which will draw attention to their resemblances to ideas previously voiced by poets and mystics, who themselves made no claim to have reached them by other than introspective means. I shall do so without dwelling too much on the absurdity of the pseudo-scientific language in which he expressed them. The reader is, however, warned that Reich's writings on orgonomy resemble other religious writings in raising problems of exegesis and hermeneutics, which make it possible for different readers to read different meanings into his writings. I gather that Reich's present day followers do not agree among themselves on the correct interpretations to be put on his theories, or on which of his writings carry his central message.

6 Orgonomy and Reich's Discovery of God

According to Reich,[1] our civilization produces two types of human beings, mechanists and mystics. Mechanists are interested in material things and the natural sciences but have no spontaneous sense of life, while mystics, on the other hand, retain a sense of life but explain it supernaturally by reference to a 'soul', which they conceive to have only an accidental, temporary and regrettable connection with the body.

The division of mankind into mechanists and mystics is the result of an unexplained 'original sin'—of which more later—which led mankind to develop a defensive armour against his own life forces. Mechanists are people who have turned completely against themselves, who have totally imprisoned their life forces within a defensive character-armour, and who have as a result no awareness of their own true nature. Mystics, on the other hand, are people who have retained glimmering

1. In this chapter I have leaned heavily on his *Selected Writings*, a work compiled and edited by Mary Boyd Higgins, who is a trustee of the Wilhelm Reich Infant Trust Fund, and have assumed that her selection constitutes an accurate and reliable statement of the Reichian position. However, as I mentioned at the end of the previous chapter, post-Reichians do not all agree among themselves and the reader should know that, when I published an article in the New York Review of Books on which this present chapter is based, I received more than one letter from Reichian therapists denying Mary Boyd Higgins's claim to be a true follower of Reich. I have however included a sufficient number of quotations from Reich to make it possible for the reader to assess for himself whether I have given an accurate account of his position.

intimations of their own life force but who deny its origin in their own bodies and locate it in a hypothetical soul.

Since both mechanists and mystics have turned against the life of the body, science and religion have failed to recognize the significance of orgasm, that bodily experience in which physical pleasure and the sense of spiritual union with the infinite are at one with each other.

Furthermore, since orgasm unites the bodily and the spiritual, understanding of its essential nature makes it possible to break down the dichotomy between the mechanical and the mystical, the natural-scientific and the religious-poetic visions of reality, and to arrive at a *Weltanschauung* which embraces both. However, anyone who succeeds, as Reich claims he did, in achieving such understanding, finds that he is in the embarrassing position of having 'stepped beyond the intellectual framework of present-day human character-structure and, with that, the civilization of the last 5,000 years.' He also incurs the hostility of both mechanists and mystics and becomes a threat to the established order. Indeed the two people who in Reich's opinion had anticipated his discoveries, Jesus Christ and Giordano Bruno (1548-1600), were both martyred. Since Bruno's life and ideas are not familiar to everyone, I should perhaps mention that he was burnt at the stake in Rome for his adherence to pantheism. 'His enthusiasm for nature, however, led him to hold an extreme form of pantheistic immanentism. God was the efficient and final cause of everything, the beginning, middle, and end, the eternal and infinite.'

The new form of thinking, feeling and experiencing which arises when the significance of orgasm is fully understood, was named by Reich 'functional', this term

2. *Oxford Dictionary of the Christian Church*. London 1957.

being chosen by him to differentiate his position from that of the mystics. It indicates that organisms function the way they do simply because it is their nature to do so and not, as the mystics maintain, at the behest of some higher purpose or power. In particular, it is the nature of man—and indeed, as Reich eventually came to believe, of all living organisms and even parts of organisms—to strive for recurrent orgasm. A rose is a rose is a rose, and an orgasm is an orgasm is an orgasm.

It was not, however, Reich's belief that the orgasms with which most members of our society are familiar were examples of the successful fusion of the mechanical and mystical. On the contrary, he held that defensive armouring against sexuality and the life forces was so wide-spread that the majority of human beings never experience orgasm in his sense of the word. 'I say on the basis of ample clinical experience that only in a few cases in our civilization is the sexual act based on love. The intervening rage, hatred, sadistic emotions and contempt are part and parcel of the love life of modern man.'

Reich's descriptions of orgasm and his interpretations and analyses of its function contain two metaphysical assumptions which at times are made explicit; that the subjective and the objective are identical; and that the whole is contained in the part.

'Man cannot feel or phantasy anything which does not actually exist in one form or another. For human perceptions are nothing but a function of objective natural processes within the organism.' (Higgins, p. 218.)

'The most general functioning principle is contained in the smallest, special functioning principle.' (*ibid.*, p. 292.)

If, to use examples used by Reich himself, we see spots in front of our eyes or have flickering sensations when we stare at the sky, these phenomena are not visual illusions but correspond to actual processes occurring in nature, and Reich devoted considerable energy and ingenuity to demonstrating that visual phenomena of this kind are really evidence of man's capacity to perceive, by reason of his vegetative harmony with nature, the bio-energy present in the sky and in nature generally and that therefore bio-energy is ubiquitous, both immanently within the perceiving organism and externally. 'Every perception is based on the consonance of a function in the outer world; that is, it is based on vegetative harmony' (Higgins, p. 219). So far as I understand this idea, it seems to me to be a pseudo-scientific formulation of the theological idea of the ubiquity of the Body of Christ; a belief which Luther held, but which Kepler, who was otherwise a devout Lutheran, got into trouble for refusing to affirm.[3]

By a similar process of reasoning, Reich persuaded himself that all the subjective impressions of yearning and excitement experienced during orgasm correspond to real 'bio-energetic' processes occurring not only in the subject's own body but also in nature at large. As a result of this 'functional identity' between the microcosm and the macrocosm, between the self and the Other, even the verbal imagery used to describe the subjective sensations occurring before, during and after orgasm can be used as valid evidence for elucidating what actually does happen during it, both inside the organism experiencing the orgasm and throughout the cosmos.

This functional mode of thinking, which, it must be emphasized, is only available to those who have suc-

3. See Arthur Koestler's *The Sleepwalkers*. London 1959.

ceeded in uniting the mystical and the mechanical, is, or so it seems to me, a pseudo-scientific version of Blake's assertion that the innocent (i.e. the unarmoured) can 'see a world in a grain of sand and a heaven in a wild flower'. According to Reich 'a thundercloud in itself has nothing to do with an ameba. Still it is possible through the observation of definite functions in the ameba to draw conclusions which are also valid for the thundercloud, for instance, the attraction which is exercised by highly-charged thunderclouds or smaller clouds just as it is exercised by an ameba on small bions.' (Bions are small packets or vesicles of bio-energy which Reich succeeded in seeing down a microscope. Higgins, p. 292.)

Since orgasm exemplifies and indeed in some sense contains within itself all living activity, analysis of its nature and course leads to complete understanding of the nature of life. The orgastic experience consists not only of tension followed by relaxation but also of a subjective sense of excitation followed by a feeling that something has been discharged. This something cannot be semen, since the feelings of tension, excitation and discharge are not confined to the genital organs and occur in women as well as in men. It must therefore be something else; at first Reich thought it was electricity, but later he decided that it was a previously unknown form of energy, 'orgone energy' or 'bio-energy', which he conceived concretely and claimed actually to have observed. Unlike Freud's libido, from which historically it derives, Reich's orgone energy is putatively an observable, 'tangible' biological phenomenon (not an explanatory psychological concept) and according to Reichians it is 'universally present and demonstrable visually, thermically, electroscopically and by means of Geiger–Müller counters' (Higgins, p. 11). It can also be stored in accumulators (orgone boxes). Almost all Reich's later researches consist of attempts, in his view consistently successful, to demonstrate the real and universal presence of bio-energy and to demonstrate its efficacy in the treatment of not only neuroses but also psychosomatic disease and cancer. He also performed experiments which demonstrated to his own satisfaction that it could be used to control the weather.

Incidentally, orgone boxes, or to give them their official name 'orgone energy accumulators' were constructed of alternating layers of steel wool and rock or glass wool, with celotex soft-board on the outside. Apparently they were the shape of a telephone box or coffin, and I am told that one did indeed feel a bit strange after being encased in one, probably on account of their poor ventilation.

Following the lead given him by quantum physics—and by Freud's idea that psychic energy exists in mobile and bound forms—Reich asserted that bio-energy exists in two forms; a mobile form consisting of mass-free pulsating vesicles (orgones) and a frozen or structured form, which has mass and is alive (bions). Mobile orgone energy is ubiquitous and identical with Primordial Cosmic Energy; structured orgone energy arises as a condensation or precipitation of mobile orgone energy first into transitional energy vesicles (bions) and later into living organisms (orgonomes). It would seem that Reich claimed both to have observed and induced experimentally the transformation of orgones into organisms, i.e. to have created life in the laboratory. One of the primary characteristics of orgones is pulsation; hence it is also the nature of orgonomes to pulsate. In doing so they generate further orgone energy, the accumulations of which are responsible for the recurrent need of all organisms for orgastic discharge.

Since an essential part of the subjective experience of orgasm is 'longing to reach out beyond the narrow sack of one's own organism' and to merge with the 'beyond of ourselves', (and not incidentally just with one's sexual partner), the orgone energy discharged during orgasm is 'functionally identical' with love. The space-occupying but weightless vesicles discovered by Reich are quanta of the love proclaimed by the mystics and denied by the mechanists. Love then is no longer an idea or an ideal but something tangible, demonstrable 'visually, thermically, electroscopically and by means of Geiger–Müller counters', and storable in orgone energy accumulators. And since orgone energy is ubiquitous and resides both inside and outside ourselves, love too is everywhere, had we but Reich's faith to see it. Love is literally what makes the world go round.

'The moving primal orgone ocean appears as the primordial mover of the heavenly bodies.' (Higgins p. 320) 'The animist Kepler, who formulated the planetary harmonic law, is, after centuries, correct with his 'vis animalis' which moves the planets. The same energy which governs the movements of animals and the growth of all living substance also actually moves the heavenly bodies.' (Higgins, p. 289) 'The physical Life Energy had been discovered in consequential pursuit of the functions of what is called 'LOVE' in the whole animal kingdom.' (Higgins, p. 355)

Incidentally, both cynics and romantics will be pleased to discover that love is blue (Higgins, p. 325).

As a result of his discovery of the functional identity

of orgone energy and love, Reich felt entitled to proclaim the unity of all antitheses.

'All boundaries between science and religion, science and art, objective and subjective, quantity and quality, physics and psychology, astronomy and religion, God and Ether, are irrevocably breaking down, being replaced by a conception of the basic unity, a basic common functional principle of all nature which branches out into the various kinds of human experience.' (Higgins, p. 423)

If the universe consisted solely of love (orgone energy), it would be a happy, joyous place, but as Reich well knew, it isn't. He had therefore to locate another form of energy, functionally identical with evil. This he found in nuclear radiation, which he conceived to be an entirely destructive, life-denying force. Fortunately, however, he succeeded in persuading himself that it could be neutralized by orgone energy, and that therefore the forces of love are, in the long run at least, more powerful than those of evil.

According to Robinson's essay on Reich[4], this conception of the universe as a battleground between life-giving orgone energy and destructive nuclear radiation is a modern, would-be scientific version of manicheism but, as I understand Reich, his position remained basically within the Judeo–Christian tradition since he also, or perhaps alternatively, postulated a destructive form of orgone energy (DOR), which becomes 'sequestered' from creative orgone energy and turns against it. This sequestered destructive energy is the force which character-

4. *The Freudian Left*, New York 1969; *The Sexual Radicals*, London 1970.

armour uses in its struggles to repress the organism's creative, orgastic strivings (Higgins, p. 455). This concept of DOR, which Reich must have derived from Freud's idea that repression is maintained by 'healthy' aggressive energy being turned back against the self (i.e. the super-ego using id-energies to combat the id), seems to me to be functionally identical' with the theological idea that the Devil is an angel cast out of heaven.

Curiously enough, DOR also manifests itself in clouds, or rather accumulations of something invisible but blighting which can overhang landscapes, especially deserts and swamps, even when the sun is shining. A 'stillness' and 'bleakness' spread over the landscape, rather well delineated against unaffected surrounding regions. The stillness is expressed in a real cessation of life expressions in the atmosphere. The birds stop singing; the frogs stop croaking. There is no sound of life anywhere. The birds fly low or hide in the trees. Animals crawl over the ground with greatly reduced motility. The leaves of the trees and the needles of the evergreens look very 'sad'; they droop, lose turgor and erectility. Every bit of sparkle or luster disappears from the lakes and the air. The trees look black, as though dying. The impression is actually that of blackness, or better, bleakness. It is not something that 'came into the landscape'. It is, rather, 'the sparkle of life that went out of the landscape' (Higgins, pp. 433–4). This is one of several passages in Reich which convince me that, deeply repressed behind his scientific character-armour, was a nature poet struggling to escape. 'The sedge has withered from the lake And no birds sing' wrote Keats; perhaps DOR and La Belle Dame Sans Merci are not as unrelated as they seem.

Reich's discovery of the objective reality of love led

him inevitably but reluctantly to God. For years 'he balked at admitting that true religion could, in spite of all its mystical distortions, be so very rational; that there could be such a thing as a rational core of all religious beliefs in an objective rational power governing the universe. He did not change his natural-scientific position; he did not now believe that a personified or absolute 'spirit' governed the world. On the contrary: 'More than ever his conviction was confirmed that there exists and acts a *physical* power in the universe at the roots of all being; a power or whatever you may call it, which finally has become accessible to being handled, directed measured, put to useful purposes by man-made tools such as thermometer, electroscope, Geiger counter, etc ... "GOD", at this point, appeared to be the perfectly logical result of man's awareness of the existence of an objective, functional logic in the universe.' (Higgins, pp 522-3. Despite the use of the third person singular, this passage is written by Reich himself.)

Although Reich has here reversed the relationship traditionally assumed to exist between God and Man—man, it appears, created God, and Reich asserts that it is he who can handle and use God, not that Man is a tool in God's hands—this passage has a curiously familiar ring about it. It has similarities with both the ideas of the 'new' theologians of the Honest to God variety who define God as 'the ground of our being' and with the form of pantheism which Wordsworth expressed openly in his Lines Composed a Few Miles Above Tintern Abbey and which he carefully eliminated from *The Prelude*.[5]

5. See Section 10 of Ernest de Selincourt's Introduction to the 'uncensored' 1805 version (London 1933).

> *And I have felt*
> *A presence that disturbs me with the joy*
> *Of elevated thoughts; a sense sublime*
> *Of something far more deeply interfused,*
> *Whose dwelling is the light of setting suns,*
> *And the round ocean and the living air,*
> *And the blue sky, and in the mind of man:*
> *A motion and a spirit, that impels*
> *All thinking things, all objects of all thought,*
> *And rolls through all things.*

(William Wordsworth. July 13th, 1798.)

Reich's account, already quoted in the previous chapter, of how his patients 'as small children ... [had] felt one with nature, with everything around them, how they felt "alive", and how all this was subsequently broken to pieces...' is also paralleled by the opening verse of Wordsworth's 'Intimations of Immortality from Recollections of Early Childhood'.

> *There was a time when meadow, grove, and stream,*
> *The earth, and every common sight,*
> *To me did seem*
> *Apparelled in celestial light,*
> *The glory and the freshness of a dream.*
> *It is not now as it hath been of yore;—*
> *Turn wherese'er I may,*
> *By night or day,*
> *The things which I have seen I now can see no more.*

Psychologically speaking, the parallels that can be drawn between Reich's 'science' of orgonomy and Wordsworth's natural religion are, I suspect, not accidental. Both lost both their parents while they were still children, and it is tempting to interpret both Reich's attempt to prove scientifically that man is at one with the cosmos and Wordsworth's ecstatic experiences of a sense of complete oneness with Nature as attempts to overcome the resulting sense of alienation and desolation. The differences between the two men and the two systems of thought, which are indeed so striking as to make any comparison seem at first sight absurd, could be attributed to the fact that Wordsworth lost his parents before puberty, whereas Reich lost his at an age when he must have already been capable of experiencing orgasm. Incidentally, there is a passage in Book II of the Prelude (lines 266–284) which suggests that Wordsworth was fully conscious of the connection between his feelings for nature and his love for his mother, whereas there is nothing in Reich's writings to suggest that he ever linked his idealization of orgasm and of matriarchy with the tragedies of his own childhood.

Despite Reich's claim to have discovered a mode of thinking which resolves all antitheses and to have demonstrated experimentally the material basis of phenomena traditionally conceived in religious, mystical or psychological terms, it must not be thought that he claimed to have solved all the riddles of the universe. On the contrary, there remained two which continued to puzzle and baffle him.

One was the differentiation of organisms into male and female. This defeated him completely. 'The division of the living orgonomes into male and female individuals still remains a riddle from the viewpoint of orgone physics' (Higgins, p. 342).

Reich's theories would indeed fit a unisex or homosexual universe as well (or as badly) as they do a heterosexual one, and it is remarkable that all his accounts of orgasm are modelled on the male's experience. He is also consistently 'phallocentric', to use Ernest Jones's word for Freud's attitude towards female sexuality, in that he always emphasizes the outgoing, thrusting, penetrative aspects of sexual desire and never enclosing, receptive longings. On the other hand, his insistence that women have sexual needs and an innate longing for orgasm as strong as the male's, coupled with his contempt for the masculine concept of sexual prowess and his emphasis on the importance of 'phallic tenderness', place him among the pioneers of women's sexual liberation. I must confess however that personally I think that there is something chilling about the way in which he explains sexual desire solely by reference to the subject's mounting internal tension without regard to the desirability—or desires—of the object—and about his emphasis on cosmic longing for union with the 'beyond' and his failure to say much about longing for the person of the loved one.

In her biography of her husband Ilse Ollendorf Reich states that in practice Reich subscribed to the Victorian double standard' of sexual morality. He had affairs in her absence but insisted on her being faithful to him. She also says that he was pathologically jealous—'I almost had to take an oath of fidelity before he would be satisfied.' In view of the well-known connections between jealousy, paranoia and unconscious homosexuality, it is also relevant that she reports that he never knowingly accepted a homosexual for treatment—'Ich will mit solchen Schweinereien nichts zu tun haben.'

The second problem to which Reich found no satisfying answer was the origin of man's tendency to turn against himself and to imprison himself in defensive armour. His failure to find one was undoubtedly a source of considerable intellectual embarrassment, since he realized clearly that his whole position depended on the assumption that man's 'original sin' of self-rejection was unnecessary and reversible.

'Still the question of how the armoring of the human animal as the only animal species [to do so] came about remains with us, unsolved, overshadowing every theoretical and practical step in education, medicine, sociology, natural science, etc. No attempt is made here to solve this problem. It is too involved. The concrete facts which possibly could provide an answer are buried in a much too distant past.' (Higgins, p. 528)

Nonetheless he does offer a solution, albeit with surprising and unusual tentativeness. It is that armouring is a side-effect of the development of reflective self-awareness. By becoming conscious and, furthermore, conscious of his capacity to be conscious, man began to treat himself as an object and to regard his urge to fuse with the beyond as a threat to his capacity to be conscious. 'In thinking about his own being and functioning, man turned involuntarily against himself; not in a destructive fashion, but in a manner which may well have been the point of origin of his armoring' (Higgins, p. 532). As Reich himself realized, this explanation of the origin of character-armour is basically a secular restatement of the religious idea that man's 'original sin' was eating of the tree of knowledge.

Although this explanation is, I suspect, correct so far as it goes, it comes as something of an anti-climax. It amounts to little more than saying that self-awareness contains within itself the risk of becoming alienated both from others and from the instinctual self, or that sur rendering oneself to one's passions and to the desire to fuse with the Other can be experienced as a threat to one's sense of identity. It seems sad that Reich should have spent such a tormented, persecuted and futile life finding out something so obvious.

It is also a conclusion which makes nonsense of his belligerence towards both the mechanists and mystics, since on his own showing they are not villains, but victims of an inescapable hazard of the human condition. A new note of tolerance which can be detected in his later writings was presumably the result of his having realized this.

7 Summing Up

Since Reich is regarded in some circles as a prophet and one of great liberators of mankind, it only remains for me to justify having, at the end of the last chapter, described his life as 'tormented, persecuted and futile'.

The evidence that Reich was a tormented personality is provided by Ilse Ollendorf Reich's biography—a disenchanted but sympathetic and loyal book which rings true throughout. His adored mother committed suicide when he was 14, his less loved father died when he was 17, his only sibling, a younger brother, died before he was thirty. From an early age he lost all contact with his origins in Bukowina. Although he became a psychoanalyst while still a medical student, his own experiences of being analyzed were unfortunate; indeed one of his analysts decamped for America without giving him any warning, leaving him, it is said, in the middle of a depression. He was restless, overactive, jealous, suspicious and possessive, smoked and drank excessively—but A. S. Neil paints a different picture, describing him as relaxed but subject to rages, and says, equally contradictorily, that he never drank to excess since drink never seemed to affect him one bit. He also suffered from two diseases, tuberculosis and eczema, which may (but on the other hand may not) have been psychosomatic. He had little sense of humour and took himself and his work dead seriously. According to A. S. Neill he found small talk unendurable—'Gesellschafts conversation just means hell to me'—and his conversation was always about his work. He also always kept a distance between himself and others. As A. S Neill says : 'Reich always put up a barrier. He addressed his fellow workers as Dr X or Dr Y and they addressed him as Dr Reich. I think that Ola Raknes of Oslo and I were the only friends and co-workers who addressed him as simply Reich!'

It seems, indeed, always to have been Reich versus the Rest and, with the exception of Freud, there seems to have been no one from whom he felt he had ever got support or inspiration. Intellectually, he seems always to have gone it alone; his writings convey no sense of dialogue with other minds; his disciples followed his lead but there is no indication that any of them contributed to the development of his thought; and his reading seems to have been directed more towards finding support for his own ideas than towards learning from others. All this suggests, I think, that he was an intrinsically lonely man, driven and tormented from within. One can only surmise that he was himself engaged in a life-long but unsuccessful struggle to escape from his own defensive armour.

He also seems to have been remarkably unself-aware. Ilse Ollendorf Reich reports that he was socially naive, over-impressed by academic titles but incapable of assessing, for instance, their different significance in the European and American scenes. As a result he often overestimated the academic standing of those who came to him for training. And, especially in someone who started life as a psychoanalyst, his obliviousness of his dynamic effect on others seems remarkable. It never seems to have occurred to him that his therapeutic successes may sometimes have been more a function of his personality than of his theories.

The fact that Reich was persecuted is shown by his

career. He was expelled from both the International Psychoanalytical Association and the communist movement. After leaving Germany for political reasons professional opposition made it impossible for him to work in Denmark and Norway. In the U.S.A. the Food and Drug Administration placed an injunction on the distribution of orgone energy accumulators and later he was imprisoned for contempt of court.

Reich seems consistently to have interpreted this persecution as evidence of the correctness of his ideas. As Ilse Ollendorf Reich emphasizes, he identified himself with Christ, whom he regarded as the archetypal 'genital character', in direct contact with cosmic orgone energy, and viewed his own life as one of martyrdom. He considered his *The Murder of Christ* to be his most important book.

Finally there are, I think, four reasons why Reich's life must be adjudged a failure and futile—this despite the fact that in his lifetime he made a stir wherever he went and that he continues to be regarded as a prophet of sexual revolution.

First, it is precisely those of his ideas by which he set most store that have to be dismissed as bizarre and absurd. His psychological ideas on defence and character-armour have, after a fashion, been assimilated by psychoanalysis and have become part of the intellectual equipment of therapists who are often unaware of their indebtedness to him, but even during his 'orthodox' psychoanalytical phase there were two features of his work and attitude which failed to have any impact on the psychoanalytical movement. These were his optimism and his therapeutic belligerence. Reich believed that the neuroses were unnecessary artefacts produced by bourgeois society and parental suppression of infantile sexual activities, but almost all analysts have followed Anna Freud in holding that 'the hope of extirpating neuroses from human life is . . . illusory.' Nor have many analysts followed Reich in being forceful and aggressive in their attacks on their patients' character-armour. Reich blitzed his patients' defences with a relentlessness that most analysts would find offensive. And those few analysts who in private will admit that on occasion they do so, are generally reluctant to recommend such a technique publicly. When I was a student at the Institute of Psycho-Analysis, London in the 1940s, my training analyst left me a typescript translation of Reich's *Der Triebhafte Character* (1925) as soon as I started treating patients, but I have no recollection of Reich being mentioned at formal lectures. And no English translation of *Der Triebhafte Character* has ever been published.

In view of the probability that Reich's contribution to the development of psychoanalysis has been greater than is generally recognized or admitted, it is of interest to note that in *Reich Speaks of Freud*,[1] Reich gives a list of establishment analysts who in his opinion understood his message but elected to remain silent.

On the other hand, Reich's would-be scientific ideas about orgones and orgone energy have rightly been rejected as fanciful. From a scientific point of view, there is something pathetic about Reich's accounts of his experiments and theories. The experiments seem to have been designed and carried out in a hopelessly amateurish and gimcrack manner with, in particular, no understanding of the need for adequate controls, while his theoriz-

---

1. This book consists of a transcript of a discussion between Reich and Kurt R. Eissler, published by the Noonday Press (1968) without the consent of either Eissler or the Sigmund Freud Archives Inc.

ing is full of the most elementary mistakes in biology and physics. One is left with the impression that Reich lacked, even as a young man, any appreciation of scientific method, and that his need to find 'tangible' things to correspond with ideas indicated some defect in his capacity for conceptual thinking.

Secondly, if one takes Reich's life and works not as a scientific career but as a spiritual progress or peculiar form of theological enquiry, his conclusions were hardly original enough to justify the torment and persecution he went through in order to reach them. The ideas that God is not the creator of the universe but is the universe and that the objective and subjective are identical crop up recurrently in the theological tradition of Western civilization. His failure to realize this provides an example of his inability to engage in dialogue with other minds. As a result, he pursued a solitary and at times heroic path, oblivious of the fact that others had explored it before him.

Thirdly, the prophetic, evangelical and often strident tone of Reich's writings has led to his being remembered as more of an extremist and revolutionary than he perhaps ever was—and certainly than he was in his later years. His intransigent advocacy of Marxism in psychoanalytical circles and of psychoanalysis within the communist movement inevitably got him into trouble with both and gave him a reputation for intellectual bloodymindedness that in retrospect hardly seems justified. Nowadays we find nothing incongruous or outrageous in attempts to reconcile Marx and Freud—indeed in certain quarters it seems to have become a fashionable exercise—or in suggestions that there may be some intrinsic connection between the social structure of a society and the psychological structure of its component members, but in the twenties and thirties in Central Europe Marxism was politics not sociology, and in the minds of the professional middle classes communism was linked with nazism, both being regarded as part of a general revolt of the masses which was threatening civilization.

Reich's unacceptability to both the communists and the analysts must have been enhanced by his assertions that a 'deep-reaching revolution of cultural living' (*The Sexual Revolution*, p. xiv) was already in progress, which was the result of neither the class dialectic of history nor the impact of psychoanalysis. This revolution, which is 'without parades, uniforms, drum or cannon salutes' and has led to 'thorough disintegration of moralistic, ascetic forms of living', Reich attributed to technological changes which were reducing the authoritarian role of fathers and loosening family ties by taking women out of the home into industry. This again is a thesis which today seems commonplace; variations of it can be found in Marcuse's accounts of 'late industrial society' and in Alexander Mitscherlich's *Society without the Father* (London 1969).

The later Reich's repudiation of his early political and sexual revolutionary position seems to have been absolute. He became virulently anti-communist and a fervent admirer of President Eisenhower, with whom indeed he believed he had a special, though secret relationship, and he came to believe that attempts to introduce sexual freedom rapidly would do more harm than good : 'If anyone had the guts and power to decree that freedom and self-regulation be established overnight, the greatest disaster in the history of mankind would inevitably swamp our lives like a flood' (Higgins, p. 512).

Fourthly, Reich's insistence on making orgasm the foundation stone of his theories renders them liable to distortion and vulgarization. Although he seems consistently throughout his life to have believed that the liberation of man depended on society's attitude towards its children and adolescents—the former should be granted the freedom to explore their own bodies and the latter the privacy to establish pre-marital relationships—his theories can be construed as a justification for adult promiscuity, which he abhorred. At the end of his life he realized this threat to his ideas and feared that his authority would be invoked to unleash 'a free-for-all fucking epidemic'. He eventually replaced the term 'orgasm' by that of 'genital embrace' and even went so far as to justify St Paul's strictures on the Flesh on the ground that 'He had to build strong dams against the pornographic, filthy, sick mind of man in sexual matters, even at the price of killing the true Christ' (Higgins, p. 514).

Bibliographical Note

Reich was an enormously prolific writer, but much of his work has never been translated into English, and much of what has is either out of print or was published in journals which were burned by the United States government. However Mary Boyd Higgins in her *Wilhelm Reich; Selected Writings* (Farrar, Straus and Cudahy, New York 1960) gives what purports to be a complete list of his writings, while Paul Edwards in his article on Reich in *The Encyclopedia of Philosophy* (Macmillan and the Free Press, New York 1967, and Collier–Macmillan, London 1967) gives an extensive though incomplete bibliography both of Reich's own writings and of the critical literature related to it.

However, to confine oneself to books which are in print and readily available, Reich's contributions to orthodox psychoanalysis can be deduced from the original versions of three papers written by him before his expulsion from the psychoanalytical movement, which are included in Robert Fliess (ed.), *The Psychoanalytic Reader* (Hogarth, London 1950). Full and indeed repetitive accounts of his theory of sex-economy and his attempts to reconcile psychoanalysis and marxism can be found in his own *Character Analysis* (Farrar, Straus and Giroux, New York 1949), *The Function of the Orgasm* (Noonday Press, New York 1942) and *The Sexual Revolution* (Farrar, Straus and Giroux, 4th revised edition, New York 1969) and in Paul Edwards's article. Extensive extracts from Reich's orgonomic 'religious' writings are given in Mary Boyd Higgins's *Selected Writings*. Reich's *The Murder of Christ* and *Listen, Little Man!* are also readily obtainable but should be avoided by anyone who wishes to retain any respect for him. Reich's *Character and Society* cannot be considered readily available.

The following works by Reich have appeared in British editions: *The Function of the Orgasm* (Panther Books, 1970), *The Sexual Revolution* (Vision Press, 1969), *Character Analysis* (Vision Press, 1969), and *Wilhelm Reich Selected Writings*, edited by Mary Boyd Higgins (Vision Press, 1961)

Bibliographical data about Reich can be found in Ilse Ollendorf Reich's *Wilhelm Reich; A Personal Biography* (St Martin's Press, New York 1969 and Elek Books, London, 1969), Paul Ritter's *Wilhelm Reich* (Ritter Press, Nottingham 1958), which was published in a limited edition and is not available, and in *Reich Speaks of Freud* (edited by Higgins and Raphael; Noonday Press, New York 1968). This book is referred to in note 1 on page 99.

Acknowledgements

For permission to quote from the works of Wilhelm Reich acknowledgement is due to Laurence Pollinger Ltd. for passages from *The Function of the Orgasm* and *Character and Society*, and to Vision Press Ltd. for passages from *The Sexual Revolution* and *Selected Writings*, edited Mary Boyd Higgins.

Fontana Books

Fontana is at present best known (outside the field of popular fiction) for its extensive lists of books on history, philosophy, and theology.

Now, however, the list is expanding rapidly to include most main subjects. New series, sometimes extensive series, of books are being specially commissioned in most main subjects – in literature politics, economics, education, geography, sociology, psychology and others. At the same time, the number of paperback reprints of books published in hardcover editions is being increased.

Further information on Fontana's present list and future plans can be obtained from:

The Non-Fiction Editor,
Fontana Books,
14 St. James's Place,
London, S.W.1.

Fontana Library of Philosophy and Theology

Bertrand Russell and the British Tradition in Philosophy
D. F. Pears

Sartre
Iris Murdoch

Symbolism and Belief
Edwyn Bevan

The Tragic Sense of Life
Miguel de Unamuno

Ethics
Letters and Papers from Prison
No Rusty Swords
Dietrich Bonhoeffer

The Humanity of God
Karl Barth

God's Grace in History
Charles Davis

Waiting on God
Simone Weil

Fontana Philosophy Classics

This series of texts and anthologies, with substantial introductions was originated by G. J. Warnock and is being continued under the editorship of A. M. Quinton.

Fontana Politics

The first two of what will be an extensive series of original books appeared in 1970. They are:

Governing Britain   A. H. Hanson and Malcolm Walles

The Commons in Transition   Edited by A. H. Hanson and Bernard Crick

Other books now available include:

The English Constitution   Walter Bagehot
Edited by R. H. S. Crossman

Asquith   Roy Jenkins

Sir Charles Dilke   Roy Jenkins

Marx and Engels: Basic Writings
Edited by Lewis S. Feuer

Democracy in America   de Tocqueville
Edited by J. P. Mayer and Max Lerner

The Downfall of the Liberal Party 1914–1935
Trevor Wilson

War and Modern Society   Alastair Buchan

Fontana Social Sciences

An extensive economics series begins publication in Spring 1971, with up to seven volumes. A sociology series is in preparation, together with a series combining sociology and literature, and sociology and history. Other books available include:

The Sociology of Modern Britain
Edited by Eric Butterworth and David Weir

People and Cities Stephen Verney

The Acquisitive Society R. H. Tawney

Memories, Dreams, Reflections C. J. Jung

African Genesis Robert Ardrey

The Territorial Imperative Robert Ardrey

The Varieties of Religious Experience William James

Lectures on Economic Principles Sir Dennis Robertson

Essays in Money and Interest Sir Dennis Robertson

Fontana History

Fontana History includes the well-known History of Europe, edited by J. H. Plumb, and the Fontana Economic History of Europe, edited by Carlo Cipolla. Four new series are in preparation. Books now available include:

The Practice of History G. R. Elton

Debates with Historians Peter Geyl

Domesday Book and Beyond F. W. Maitland

The English Reformation A. G. Dickens

The Nation State and Self-Determination Alfred Cobban

Europe and The French Revolution Albert Sorel

Russia 1917: The February Revolution George Katkov

The Downfall of the Liberal Party Trevor Wilson

The Trial of Charles I C. V. Wedgwood

The King's Peace 1637–1641 C. V. Wedgwood

The King's War 1641–1647 C. V. Wedgwood

Fontana Literature

Literature may well provide the largest single section of the expanding Fontana list. In preparation is an extensive critical history of English, American, and Commonwealth literature, and a series on literature and sociology. Books now available include:

Axel's Castle Edmund Wilson

Sartre Iris Murdoch

The Brontë Story Margaret Lane

Early Victorian Novelists David Cecil

The Stricken Deer David Cecil

Modern Australian Writing Edited by Geoffrey Dutton

Modern Poets on Modern Poetry Edited by James Scully